Make Amazing Toy and Game Gadgets

Amy Pinchuk

Illustrated by Allan Moon and Tina Holdcroft

HarperTrophy®
An Imprint of HarperCollinsPublishers

First published in Canada by Greey de Pencier Books Inc. in 2001
First United States edition published by HarperCollins Children's Books, a
division of HarperCollins*Publishers,* in 2001

"Popular Mechanics for Kids" is a trademark of Hearst Communications, Inc.

Make Amazing Toy and Game Gadgets
Text copyright © 2001 by Amy Pinchuk
Illustrations copyright © 2001 by Allan Moon
Illustrations copyright © 2001 by Tina Holdcroft

Also available: *Make Cool Gadgets for Your Room*

Dedication
Dedicated with a smile to my teacher Dr. Peter Peet Silvester.

Acknowledgments
Thank you, Sheba, for your inspiration and guidance in writing these books,
Keltie and Kat for editing them, and Word & Image for making them look
great. Thanks to the following for all of their help: Mark, Matthew, Rachel,
Paul, Daniel, David, Josh, Lenny, Dad, Mom, and R. Paknys. I also gratefully
acknowledge the following contributions: Bill Bowden and his website
"Bowden's Hobby Circuits" for his Fading Red Eyes circuit for Cool Shades.
The Pinhole Camera design was modified from a design published by Kodak.
Lightning Technologies Inc. graciously supplied the Lightning and Aircraft
photo. Finally I would like to thank all of those "experts" out there who
replied to my e-mail queries on many of the subjects contained in this book.

Library of Congress catalog number: 00-108171
ISBN 0-688-17797-2
ISBN 0-688-17726-3 (pbk.)

Design & Art Direction: Word & Image Design Studio
Illustrations for all sidebars, Try This!, Zoom in on the Mechanics, Troubleshoot
It, and Building Tips, plus pages 4 (top and on left), 5 (bottom), 6, 7, 16, 22
(top left), 33 (bottom right), 34, 44, 54 (2 on right): Tina Holdcroft
All other illustrations: Allan Moon
Photography: Ray Boudreau

Printed in Hong Kong

1 2 3 4 5 6 7 8 9 10

Contents

Build Amazing Toys and Games, Now!

Put your building cap on, roll up your sleeves, and make some awesome toys and games. All of these nifty gadgets are made of buzzers that buzz, parts that move, and lights that flash. So they're fun to build and play around with. What's more, they'll make you the most fun-to-be-with kid on the block.

Outta Sight Light Box

Made from an ordinary matchbox, this little treasure box lights up when you open it. It makes a great spy flashlight, cool greeting card, or just a funky place to stash stuff.

Buzz Off Game

Make a game that requires a steady hand. Move the wand along the wire. But don't touch the wire or — bzzzzt — you'll have to buzz off and let the next person take a turn.

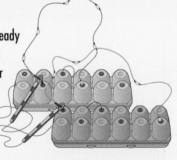

Flashy Jewelry

Light up your life — or someone else's — with a handmade piece of jewelry. Powered by a battery, the lights flash on and off to reveal the wearer's inner glow.

Cool Shades

Glasses so cool you can wear them in the dark. You create the circuit yourself that makes the lights flash on and off, slowly or quickly — it's your choice.

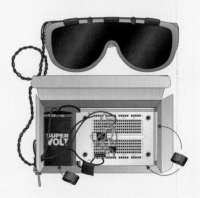

Spy Camera

A small and silent pinhole camera — made out of cardboard, paper, and glue, and using real film.

4

Start by choosing a cool gadget that you want to make. Then carefully read through all the step-by-step instructions. This will give you an idea of what you're going to do and what to expect along the way.

■ Your personal guide leads you through the tough parts and tells you what to watch out for as you build.

■ **Test This!** directions help you test the gadget as you go to make sure it's in perfect working order every step of the way.

■ **Zoom In on the Mechanics** gives you the inside scoop on how each gadget works.

■ Step-by-step pictures and instructions show you how to make each gadget.

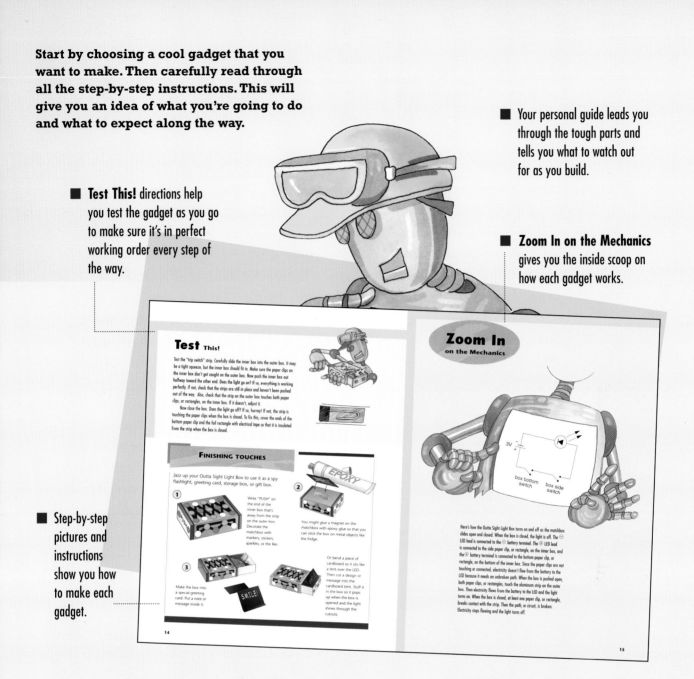

Once you've chosen a project, take a good look at **Tools & Stuff You Need** on the first page of the activity. Chances are you'll be able to find most of these things around your home, and you'll have a few things to buy from local hardware or electronic stores.

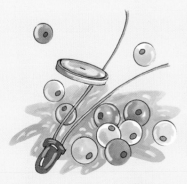

Gather up what you've got at home, make a shopping list, and buy what you need. If you can't find exactly what's called for, try to find something similar. For example, use Bristol™ board instead of index cards. But when it comes to electrical stuff like wires, batteries, and electrical tape, play it safe by using exactly what's listed. Check out **The "What's That?" Glossary** on page 60 and **How-to Tips** on page 57 to find out more about what things are and how to use them. Get going and have fun!

Put Safety First

When it comes to building mechanical gadgets and working with electrical gizmos, pros always put safety first. The pros check and test what they're building every step of the way. They also make sure their finished product is neat and tidy so it is safe to use.

All of the gadgets described in this book are perfectly safe to make. The step-by-step instructions for building them are based on the methods of the pros. When extra safety caution is needed for certain steps, the instructions tell you to wear safety goggles or to get an adult to help. The activities in this book are for kids at least nine years old. Keep all materials out of the reach of younger children.

Here are a few golden rules to help you play it safe:
- Handle all tools with care.
- All the gadgets use regular batteries. Use only the batteries listed. NEVER try to make or use any of the gadgets with other power sources like the plug-in outlets in your home or larger batteries. That's a double D: dumb and dangerous!
- Read over and follow any directions that come with the stuff you're working with such as glue, buzzers, batteries, and resistors.
- Take special care when you're working with glue. When using drills, X-Acto knives, and other cutting tools, always work with an adult. Never drill or cut toward your body or your hands. Make sure you don't damage any furniture or surfaces around you.
- If you're not sure about something, ask an adult for help.

Outta Sight Light Box

Turn an ordinary matchbox into an Outta Sight Light Box that lights up when you open it. It makes a great spy flashlight, cool greeting card, or funky storage or gift box for special stuff.

Tools & Stuff You Need

- a small matchbox (about 5.5 cm x 3.5 cm, or 2 in x 1$\frac{1}{4}$ in)
- small 3-volt "coin" battery
- a 1.5- to 3-volt LED with long leads about 3 cm (1$\frac{1}{4}$ in)
- aluminum pie plate, toothpicks
- 2 paper clips, ruler, pencil, black marker, pin
- scissors
- electrical tape, 5-minute epoxy glue
- needle-nose pliers or tweezers
- markers, stickers, or sparkles
- small magnet (optional)

Add paper clips to clip on the light-making gear.

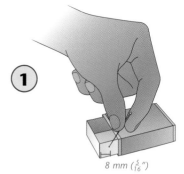

① Use the pin to make a small hole in the side of the inner box as shown.

8 mm ($\frac{5}{16}$")

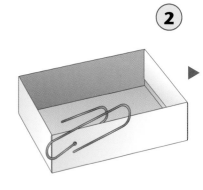

② Insert a paper clip through the hole to attach it to the side of the box as shown. If the side of the box is too thin for a paper clip, skip this step.

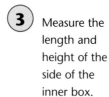

③ Measure the length and height of the side of the inner box.

length

height

Draw two rectangles on the pie plate, each 1 cm ($\frac{3}{8}$ in) less than the box length and 3 mm ($\frac{1}{8}$ in) shorter than the height. Cut them out.

Solar Polar
Fireworks

There are some mysterious lights in nature that can turn on and off all on their own. The Northern Lights, also called the Aurora Borealis, are amazing colorful ribbons of light that often dance in the nighttime sky over the North Pole. Long ago, Inuit people thought the shimmery lights were warnings from the gods about bad things to come. But now scientists know that this polar light show is caused by heat around the sun, which creates charged particles that travel towards the Earth. Some of these charged particles get trapped in the Earth's atmosphere near the Magnetic North and South Poles. And when they bump into air molecules, they give off green, red, violet and blue lights. Just call them solar, polar fireworks!

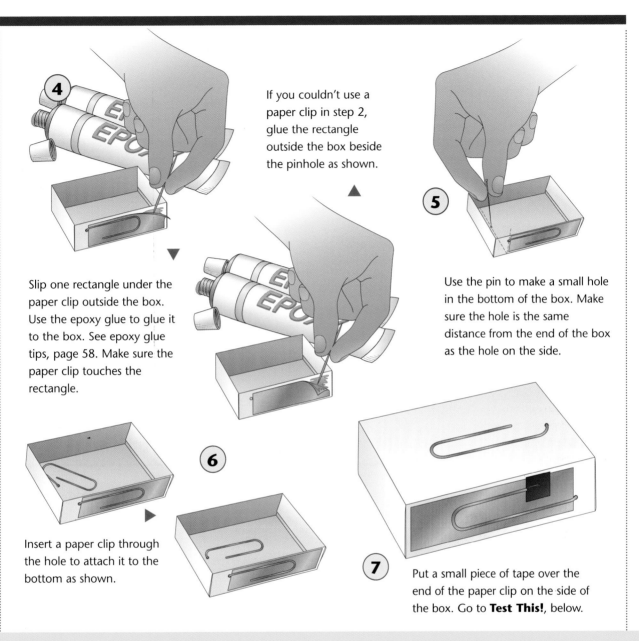

4

If you couldn't use a paper clip in step 2, glue the rectangle outside the box beside the pinhole as shown. ▲

Slip one rectangle under the paper clip outside the box. Use the epoxy glue to glue it to the box. See epoxy glue tips, page 58. Make sure the paper clip touches the rectangle.

▼

5

Use the pin to make a small hole in the bottom of the box. Make sure the hole is the same distance from the end of the box as the hole on the side.

6

Insert a paper clip through the hole to attach it to the bottom as shown. ▶

7

Put a small piece of tape over the end of the paper clip on the side of the box. Go to **Test This!**, below.

Test This!

Now that the paper clips are in place, does the matchbox still slide open and closed? Test it out. Put the matchbox back together. Then push the inner box to open and close the matchbox. If it still slides, everything is A-OK! Remove the outer box and go to the next step. If not, try to adjust the position of the paper clip to help the inner box slide. If it still doesn't slide, remove the side paper clip. Go back to step 3 of Gear Up for Light to redo the steps, following the instructions for what to do if you can't use a paper clip.

9

Set up the battery to power up the matchbox.

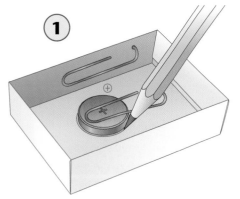

1 Slip the battery under the bottom paper clip inside the box as shown. Use the pencil to mark the position of the battery on the box.

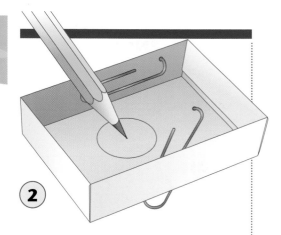

2 Remove the battery and slide the paper clip to the side. Draw a dot in the center of the battery tracing.

3 Use the pin to make two holes 3mm ($\frac{1}{8}$ in) apart around the center point of the battery. Make the holes on a diagonal line toward the corner as shown.

4 Check the instructions that came with the LED to see which lead is negative $\ominus$. It's usually the shorter lead. Color it with the black marker to help you identify it later. Go to **Test This!**, below.

Test This!

Test the LED and the battery. Slip the battery between the LED leads so the $\ominus$ lead lines up with the $\ominus$ battery terminal and $\oplus$ lead lines up with the $\oplus$ battery terminal. Squeeze the leads against the terminals. Does the LED light up? If so, everything is working. If not, make sure the LED leads and the battery are lined up properly. Also, check that the $\ominus$ lead is touching only the center part of the $\ominus$ battery terminal — the outer rim is part of the $\oplus$ terminal. If the LED still doesn't light up, the LED or the battery needs to be replaced.

Let there be light. All right!

INSTALL THE LIGHT

Get stitching. Sew a light into the box!

1 Stand the LED in the corner of the box as shown. Check that the ⊕ lead can wrap around the paper clip on the side of the box and the ⊖ lead can reach the tracing of the battery. Make a pinhole for the ⊖ lead close to the LED as shown.

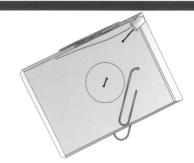

2 Thread the ⊖ lead through the pinhole out the bottom of the box. Then thread it through the pinholes in the center of the box to make a stitch between the pinholes as shown.

3 Connect the ⊕ lead to the paper clip on the side of the box. Twist it under and around the loop.

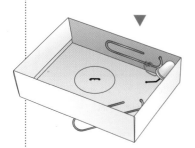

If you used a piece of aluminum instead of a paper clip, make two pinholes through the aluminum and sew the ⊕ lead through the side of the box and the aluminum.

4 Use electrical tape to cover the ⊖ lead on the bottom outside of the box. Make sure the tape insulates the lead from the paper clip to stop metal objects from touching the lead and causing a "short circuit."

Ice Age Snapshots

Thousands of years ago, people painted pictures on cave walls, and today their paintings shed light on what their life was like in the Ice Age. What's cool is that two of the most famous painted caves were discovered by kids. In 1879, the Altimara Cave, in Spain, which features lifesize paintings of bulls and horses, was discovered by five-year-old Maria de Sautuola when she wandered away from her father and slipped into a cave near their house. Sixty-one years later in France, the Lascaux caves were discovered by four teenage boys who went looking for their lost dog. Not only did they find the dog, but they also found cave paintings of Ice Age animals running and swimming. If kids in the future discovered your Light Box thousands of years from now, what could it tell them about your life today?

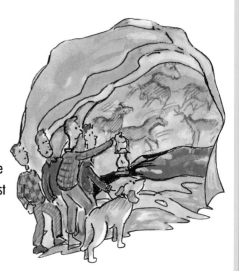

Power up your Outta Sight Light Box.

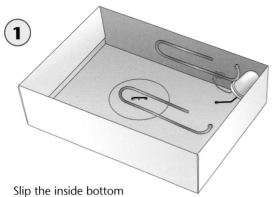

1 Slip the inside bottom paper clip back in place so it surrounds the stitch.

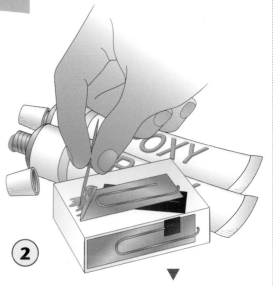

2 Slip the second foil rectangle under the paper clip. Using epoxy glue, glue the rectangle to the outside bottom of the box as shown.

3 Use a small piece of electrical tape to cover the end of the paper clip as shown.

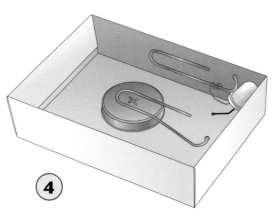

4 Slide the battery under the paper clip so the ⊖ terminal faces down and presses against the stitch. Go to **Test This!**, page 13.

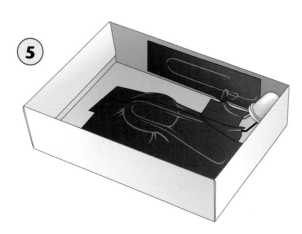

5 Once you've tested the circuit, cover the battery and paper clips with electrical tape so they won't get knocked about by stuff you will put in the box.

Test This!

Test the circuit between the LED and the battery. Use a bent paper clip or stripped wire to touch the rectangles or paper clips on the side and bottom of the box at once. See wire stripping tips, page 59. Does the light go on? If so, hurray! Everything is working. If not, check that all the connections are good. Also, check that the stitch in the $\ominus$ LED lead is pressing against the $\ominus$ battery terminal. Make sure the stitch is not touching the $\oplus$ rim around the $\ominus$ terminal.

> Right on! The light's on!

TRIP SWITCH STRIP

Line the box with a "trip switch" that will turn the light on and off as you slide the box open and closed.

1 Measure the width and height of the outer box and add them together for length.

▼

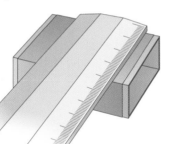

Measure the distance from the bottom paper clip to the end of the box and subtract 3 mm ($\frac{1}{8}$ in) for width.

▼

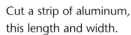

Cut a strip of aluminum, this length and width.

2 Check that the strip is long enough to go across the box and up the inside wall as shown.

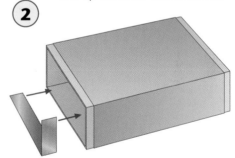

3 Use the epoxy glue to glue the strip on the outer box where shown. Make sure both rectangles on the inner box touch the strip when the inner box slides out of the outer box. Keep the surface of the strip free of glue. Let the glue dry for 15 minutes. Go the **Test This!**, page 14.

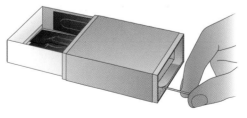

Test This!

Test the "trip switch" strip. Carefully slide the inner box into the outer box. It may be a tight squeeze, but the inner box should fit in. Make sure the paper clips on the inner box don't get caught on the outer box. Now push the inner box out halfway toward the other end. Does the light go on? If so, everything is working perfectly. If not, check that the strips are still in place and haven't been pushed out of the way. Also, check that the strip on the outer box touches both paper clips, or rectangles, on the inner box. If it doesn't, adjust it.

Now close the box. Does the light go off? If so, hurray! If not, the strip is touching the paper clips when the box is closed. To fix this, cover the ends of the bottom paper clip and the foil rectangle with electrical tape so that they are insulated from the strip when the box is closed.

FINISHING TOUCHES

Jazz up your Outta Sight Light Box to use it as a spy flashlight, greeting card, storage box, or gift box.

1

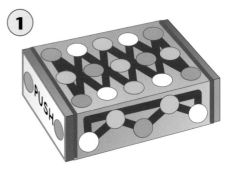

Write "PUSH" on the end of the inner box that's away from the strip on the outer box. Decorate the matchbox with markers, stickers, sparkles, or the like.

2

You might glue a magnet on the matchbox with epoxy glue so that you can stick the box on metal objects like the fridge.

3

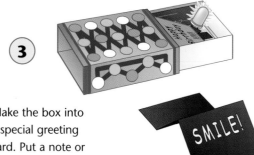

Make the box into a special greeting card. Put a note or message inside it.

Or bend a piece of cardboard so it sits like a tent over the LED. Then cut a design or message into the cardboard tent. Stuff it in the box so it pops up when the box is opened and the light shines through the cutouts.

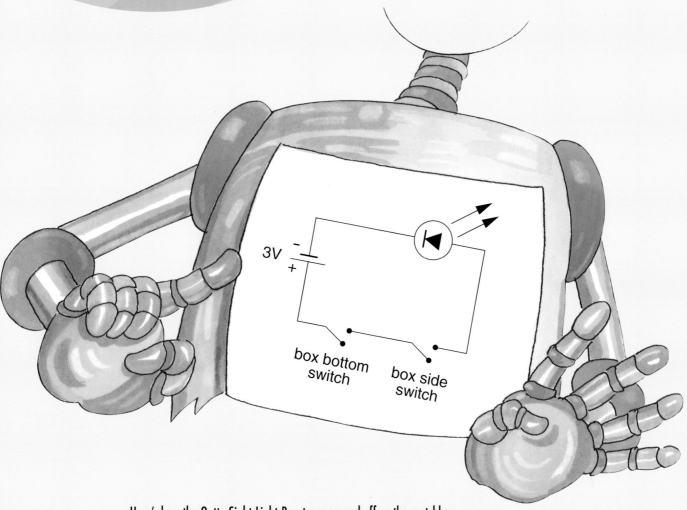

Here's how the Outta Sight Light Box turns on and off as the matchbox slides open and closed. When the box is closed, the light is off. The ⊖ LED lead is connected to the ⊖ battery terminal. The ⊕ LED lead is connected to the side paper clip, or rectangle, on the inner box, and the ⊕ battery terminal is connected to the bottom paper clip, or rectangle, on the bottom of the inner box. Since the paper clips are not touching or connected, electricity doesn't flow from the battery to the LED because it needs an unbroken path. When the box is pushed open, both paper clips, or rectangles, touch the aluminum strip on the outer box. Then electricity flows from the battery to the LED and the light turns on. When the box is closed, at least one paper clip, or rectangle, breaks contact with the strip. Then the path, or circuit, is broken. Electricity stops flowing and the light turns off.

Flashy Jewelry

Want to light up your life? Or make a gift for your mother, sister, or sweetheart for a special day or birthday? This Flashy Jewelry is guaranteed to do the trick. Handmade by you and powered by a battery, it flashes on and off to reveal the wearer's inner glow.

Tools & Stuff **You Need**

- scissors
- needle-nose pliers or tweezers
- small 3-volt "coin" battery
- 1.5- to 3-volt blinking LED with long leads about 3 cm (1$\frac{1}{4}$ in)
- plastic beads, non-metallic thread
- toothpicks
- 5-minute epoxy glue
- masking tape, black marker
- thin wire (optional)

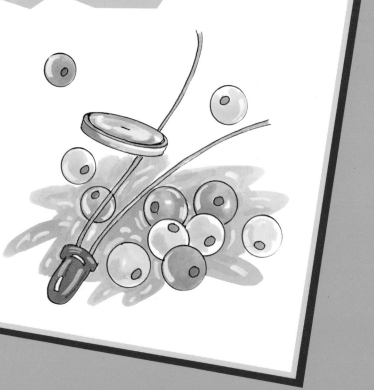

Turn a blinking LED into a flashy jewel.

1 Check the instructions that came with the LED to see which lead is negative ⊖. It's usually the shorter lead. Color it with the black marker to help you identify it later.

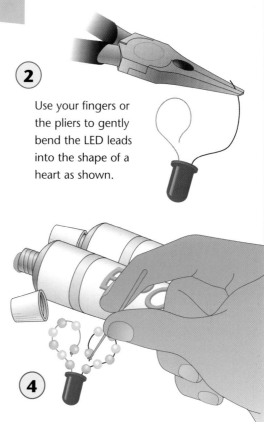

2 Use your fingers or the pliers to gently bend the LED leads into the shape of a heart as shown.

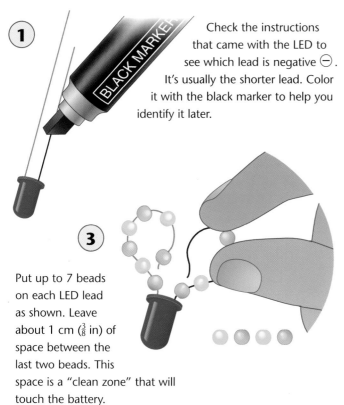

3 Put up to 7 beads on each LED lead as shown. Leave about 1 cm ($\frac{3}{8}$ in) of space between the last two beads. This space is a "clean zone" that will touch the battery.

4 Dab epoxy glue on the end beads as shown, so they don't fall off. See epoxy glue tips, page 58. Make sure the epoxy doesn't get on the "clean zone." Let the epoxy dry for 2 hours. Go to **Test This!** below.

Test This!

Test the flashy jewel circuit before you glue the battery in place. Line up the battery with the LED so the ⊖ battery terminal faces the ⊖ LED lead. Slip the battery between the LED leads and place it so it makes good contact with the leads. Does the LED flash? If so, hurray! The circuit works just fine. If not, check for epoxy glue on the LED leads and scrape any off with a scissors blade. Pinch the leads together to improve their contact with the battery. Also, check that the ⊖ lead is contacting the ⊖ battery terminal and that the positive ⊕ lead is contacting the ⊕ terminal. If the LED still doesn't flash, the battery or the LED needs to be replaced.

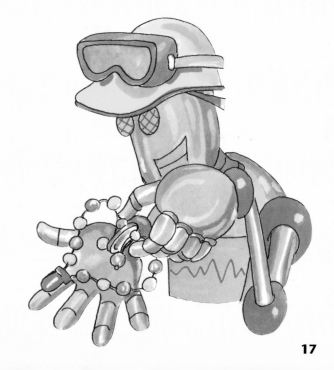

Light up your jewel and flash on.

1 Put small pieces of masking tape on each battery terminal as shown. The tape will keep the battery clear of epoxy glue and stop the LED from flashing as you build.

Use a toothpick to apply epoxy glue on the end bead of the ⊖ LED lead and the lower part of ⊖ battery terminal as shown.

2

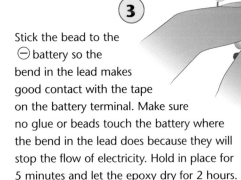

3 Stick the bead to the ⊖ battery so the bend in the lead makes good contact with the tape on the battery terminal. Make sure no glue or beads touch the battery where the bend in the lead does because they will stop the flow of electricity. Hold in place for 5 minutes and let the epoxy dry for 2 hours.

4 Carefully remove the tape from the battery terminals. Try not to bend the LED leads. Does this make the LED flash? If so, great! Go to step 5. If not, go to **Troubleshoot It**, page 19.

Curse of a **Flashy Diamond**

More than 4000 years ago, or so the story goes, the Koh-i-noor diamond was found in India. It flashed brilliantly and tipped the gemstone scales at a whopping 108 carats. But its real claim to fame is its mighty curse: something very bad will happen to any man who owns it, but any woman who owns it will rule the world. True to its reputation, male emperors, noblemen, and thieves who owned the Koh-i-noor were murdered or died grisly deaths. One man stole it by swapping turbans with the owner, who had hidden it in his turban. When the thief unraveled the stolen turban and saw the diamond, he gasped, "Koh-i-noor," which means "mountain of light." The thief was murdered soon after, but the name stuck. Today, the Koh-i-noor diamond is set in the crown of England's Queen Mother, who has lived a long, prosperous life for over 100 years.

What a mountain of light!

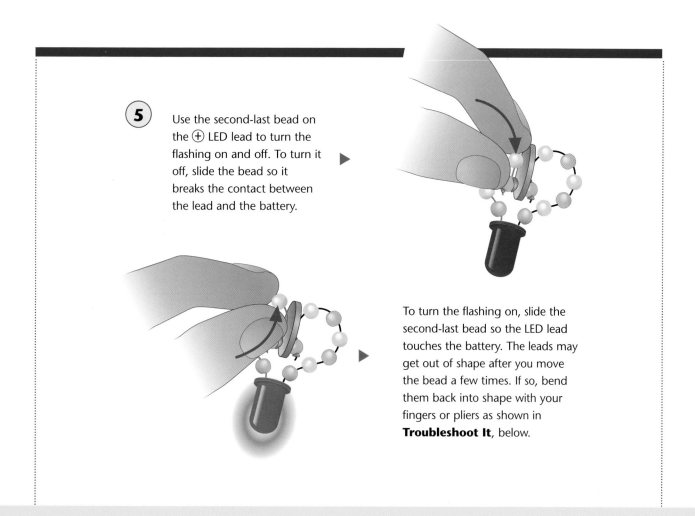

5 Use the second-last bead on the ⊕ LED lead to turn the flashing on and off. To turn it off, slide the bead so it breaks the contact between the lead and the battery.

To turn the flashing on, slide the second-last bead so the LED lead touches the battery. The leads may get out of shape after you move the bead a few times. If so, bend them back into shape with your fingers or pliers as shown in **Troubleshoot It**, below.

Troubleshoot It

After you remove the tape in step 4, the LED leads should touch the battery to make the LED flash on and off. The ⊖ lead should touch the battery close to where the end of it is glued to the battery and the ⊕ lead should automatically press against the battery. If the LED doesn't flash, one or both of these contacts aren't being made. But don't panic. Check that the clean zones on the leads and battery are clean and free of glue. Then use the pliers to carefully rebend both leads as shown, so they press against the battery's clean zones.

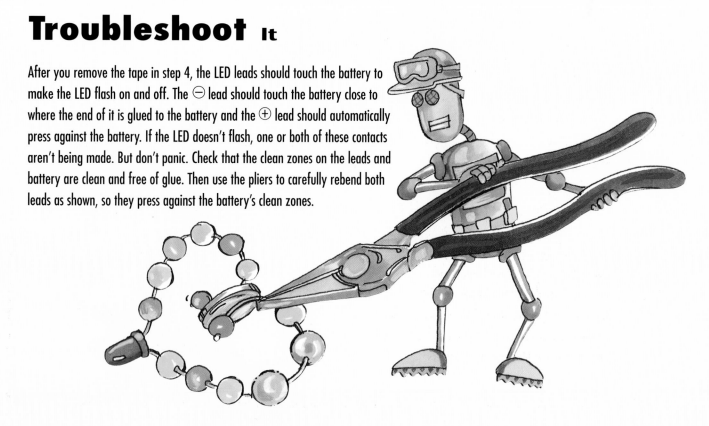

Break out the beads and give the Flashy Jewelry your personal touch.

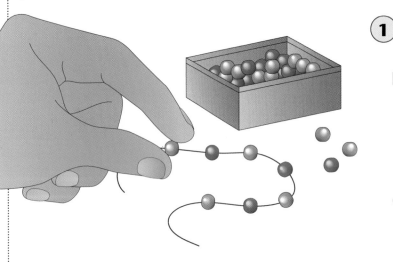

1 Make a necklace by stringing beads on the thread. Make sure the thread is not wire thread, because wire could conduct electricity away from the LED.

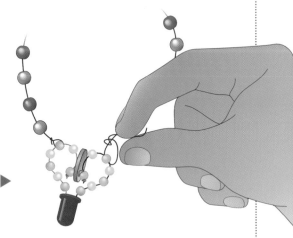

2 Tie the necklace to the third-last beads on the LED leads. Make sure you don't tie it to the second-last bead on the ⊕ lead, because this bead switches the jewelry on and off. Be careful not to bend the leads out of shape and make sure the beads on either side of the battery do not move and ruin the contact. Go to **Test This!**, page 21.

"Purrfectly" Electric

Around 600 BC an ancient Greek philosopher, or thinker, discovered that the gemstone amber brought out his pet cat's "magnetic" personality. When the philosopher rubbed amber on the cat's fur, an awesome thing happened. The rubbed amber began to attract lightweight objects and the objects stuck to it. We now know that this phenomenon was caused by static electricity. As the amber rubbed the fur, ⊖ charges in the fur moved into the amber. Then the amber began to attract things that had a ⊕ charge. The same thing happens when your stockinged feet rub on a carpet and you then give an electric shock to an unsuspecting friend. The cat didn't end up with any claim to fame. But the word *electric* was coined from the Greek word for amber.

Test This!

Now that the jewel is hanging from the necklace, does it still work? Put on the necklace and test it out. Move the second-last bead on the ⊕ LED lead back and forth to turn the LED on and off. Does it flash? If so, congrats! If not, the leads may have gotten bent out of shape. See **Troubleshoot It**, page 19, to bend them back.

Zoom In
on the Mechanics

Nowadays, some lights and batteries are so small that they can easily be used to make jewelry. The Flashy Jewelry uses a very simple circuit made only of the two LED leads and the battery. (The blinking LED is specially designed to blink on and off without a special circuit.) When the ⊖ LED lead touches the ⊖ battery terminal and the ⊕ lead touches the ⊕ battery terminal, the LED turns on and starts to flash. When one of these contacts is broken, the LED turns off and the flashing stops. You break the contact by moving a plastic bead, which does not conduct or carry electricity, between the ⊕ lead and the battery. So turning the Flashy Jewelry on and off is as simple as moving a bead!

21

Design

Your Own Flashy Jewelry

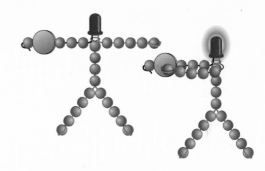

Want to make your own flashy jewelry designs with LEDs and batteries? Just follow these simple rules and have fun!

1 Make sure the battery provides the required voltage for the LED you're using.

2 Set up the $\oplus$ LED lead so it touches the $\oplus$ battery terminal.

3 Set up the $\ominus$ LED lead so it touches the $\ominus$ battery terminal.

4 Use masking tape to keep all contact areas on the LED and battery clean while you are gluing. Then take the tape off.

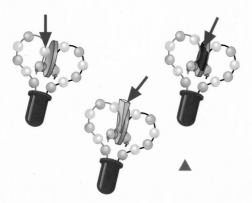

5 To turn off the flashing LED, break the contact between one of the LED leads and the battery terminal. One way to do this is to slide an object that does not conduct electricity, such as a plastic bead, paper, tape or wood, between them.

6 Another way to turn off the flashing LED is to move or bend the lead away from the battery. For example, a piece of jewelry shaped like a person may hold the battery in one hand. When the hands are pressed together, the flashing LED is on. When the hands are moved apart, it turns off.

7 To turn on the flashing LED, complete the loop between the LED leads and the battery by connecting one lead (or a wire connected to the lead) to the battery terminal of the same sign.

8 To make fancy jewelry, extend the length of the leads by connecting wire to them, such as solid core wire, totally stripped wire, or even a paper clip. See connecting wires tips, page 58. Make sure the leads and the wire make good contact with each other. Twist them together or thread them through a narrow bead together.

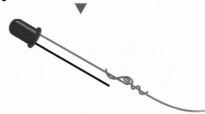

9 Add as many objects made of materials that do not conduct electricity, such as beads, paper, tape, or wood, as you want as long as they are not part of the electric circuit when the flashing LED is on.

10 Do not puncture or hammer the battery, or expose it to heat or an open flame.

11 The end of the LED is the brightest part. Try to design your jewelry so the end of the LED points out.

Spy Camera

Would you believe that you can make a camera out of cardboard, paper, and glue that uses real film and takes awesome photos? Make this pinhole camera and see. It's small enough to stash in your pocket, and it won't make a sound as you snap away. So it's a perfect spy camera and great for taking pictures of sleeping animals!

Tools & Stuff You Need

- safety goggles
- 110 cartridge color film
- X-Acto or sharp knife
- # 10 sewing needle
  (a very thin 0.3 mm
  ($\frac{1}{75}$ in) needle used
  for sewing beads)
- wire cutters
- pliers
- scissors

- black, thin cardboard or Bristol™ board
- black, thick cardboard
(If you don't have black, color it with a black marker until no white shows.)
- aluminum pie plate
- wire paper clip
- safety pin
- black electrical or hockey tape
- white glue
- ruler
- pencil
- ballpoint pen (fine point)

MAKE THE CAMERA BODY

Get set to turn a thin piece of cardboard into the body of a working camera.

(1)

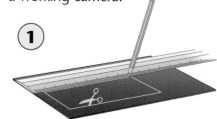

Draw a rectangle exactly 3.2 x 8.8 cm ($1\frac{1}{4}$ x $3\frac{1}{2}$ in) on the thin cardboard. Cut it out.

(2)

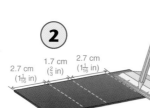

2.7 cm ($1\frac{1}{16}$ in) 1.7 cm ($\frac{2}{3}$ in) 2.7 cm ($1\frac{1}{16}$ in)

Draw three fold lines on the rectangle exactly as you see here.

(3)

Just build it!

Make the cardboard easier to fold by scratching the X-acto knife along the fold lines. But don't cut all the way through!

(4)

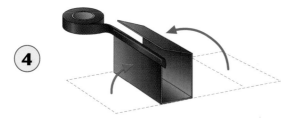

Fold the cardboard to make a rectangular tube. Make sure the two edges meet at the corner without any gap or overlap. Tape the edges together with the black tape.

(5)

Cover this joint completely with an extra piece of tape to keep unwanted light from seeping into the camera body.

The Whole World Is Upside Down

It sounds crazy, but all the photos your pinhole camera takes are upside down! But you'd never know it. Why not? What do you do when you look at an upside-down photo? You automatically turn it right side up! The images that light creates on the film are upside down because when light comes off an object, it travels in straight lines. Only some of this light goes through the pinhole (see page 27). The light from the top of the object goes through the pinhole and strikes the bottom of the film. Likewise, the light from the bottom of the object goes through the pinhole and hits the top of the film. So the image of the object gets flipped upside down!

Make the aperture and holder

Take a pie plate and a sewing needle and create a pinhole window that will capture your shots of the world.

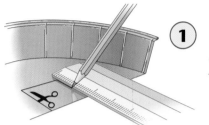

1 Draw a 1.6 x 1.6 cm ($\frac{5}{8}$ x $\frac{5}{8}$ in) square on a flat part of the pie plate. Cut it out.

2 Find the square's center by drawing two straight, diagonal lines across the square, from corner to corner. The center is where the diagonal lines meet.

3 Put the square on a flat, hard surface like a table. Hold the needle with the pliers as you see here. Use the needle tip to poke a small hole through the center of the square. Don't push the rest of the needle through. This pinhole is the aperture of the camera — the smaller the hole the sharper the photos!

4 Draw a 3.3 x 5.1 cm ($1\frac{3}{4}$ x 2 in) rectangle on the thick black cardboard. Cut it out.

5 Draw a line 1 cm ($\frac{3}{8}$ in) below the top of the rectangle and another line 1 cm ($\frac{3}{8}$ in) above the bottom. Then draw a line 1.9 cm ($\frac{3}{4}$ in) away from the rectangle's left side and another line 1.9 cm ($\frac{3}{4}$ in) from the right side. Draw straight diagonal lines through the center of the square. Extend the lines out to the edges of the rectangle.

6 Cut out the square carefully with the X-Acto knife. Now you should have a window. Ta-da! You've just made a holder for the aperture. Color its inside edges with the black marker.

7 Without bending or folding the aperture, carefully place it in the window. Center the pinhole in the window by lining up the diagonal lines with the corners of the square.

8 Tape the edges of the aperture to the cardboard. Cover all of its foil edges with the black tape to stop unwanted light from getting in. Do the same with the outer edges of the holder.

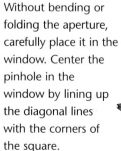 

It doesn't take much to shut unwanted light out of your camera. A piece of black cardboard will do the trick!

1 Draw two 3.3 x 3.3 cm ($1\frac{1}{4}$ x $1\frac{1}{4}$ in) squares on the thin black cardboard. Cut them out.

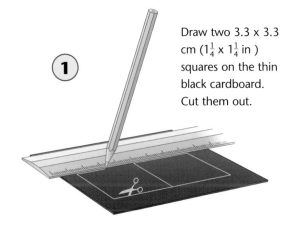

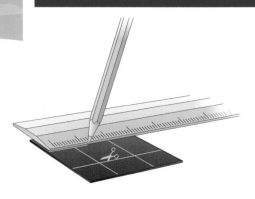

2 Make one square into a window by drawing four lines, each 1 cm ($\frac{3}{8}$ in) from one edge of the square. Cut it out with the X-Acto knife.

3 Make the second square into a U-shape by drawing a line 0.6 cm ($\frac{1}{4}$ in) above the bottom of the square, 0.6 cm ($\frac{1}{4}$ in) from the right side, and 0.6 cm ($\frac{1}{4}$ in) from the left side. Cut out the U shape with the X-Acto knife. Way to go! You've made a spacer that will hold the shutter.

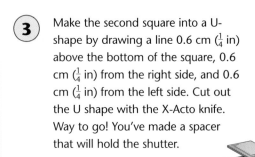

4

WHITE GLUE

Glue the spacer to the square with the window.

5

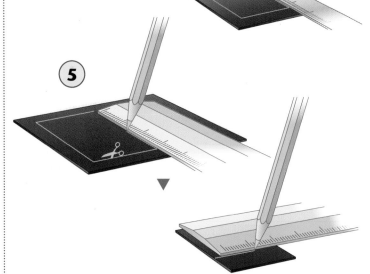

Draw and cut a 2.1 x 3.3 cm ($\frac{7}{16}$ x $1\frac{1}{4}$ in) rectangle out of the thin black cardboard. Congrats — this is the shutter! Draw a line across it 1 cm ($\frac{3}{8}$ in) above the bottom. This line marks how high to pull up the shutter when you take a picture.

6 The shutter should slide up and down in the spacer. Test it out. If it doesn't slide easily, trim it slightly with the scissors.

Zoom In
on the Mechanics

A camera has three main parts that work together:
- **film** *that pictures are made on*
- *a window, or* **aperture**, *that lets light shine on the film*
- *a* **shutter** *that stops light from shining on the film*

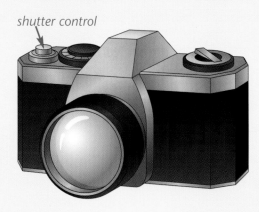

shutter control

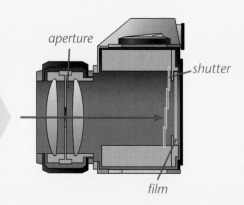

aperture

shutter

film

(1) Lights, Camera, Action!

Film is designed to use light to record an image of an object. All objects — your dog, your skateboard, and even you — reflect light, either from the sun or artificial light. When a camera shutter opens, it lets this reflected light shine through the aperture onto the film. The light leaves an image of the object on the film, which can be developed with chemicals. Then the image is printed on paper and — voilà! You've got a photo of your dog, your skateboard, or you.

(3) Perfect Lighting

Say, for example, you were using a standard camera to take a shot of your friend skateboarding on a sunny day. To get the perfect amount of light on the film (at film speed ISO 100), you'd make the aperture fairly small, about 3 mm ($\frac{1}{8}$ in) wide, and set the shutter to open for a very short period of time, about 1 100th of a second. That means your camera has to open and close the shutter faster than the blink of an eye!

(2) The Tricks of Pics

The tricky part of taking pictures is getting just the right amount of light on the film to record an image. If too much light gets on the film, your photos will be all white. But if too little light gets on it, they will be too dark. The aperture and the shutter allow you to control this amount of light. The larger you make the aperture, the more light you let in. Likewise, the longer you leave the shutter open, the more light you let in.

(4) The W-hole Secret

So how does this pinhole camera work without any automatic gizmos — just cardboard, tape, and glue? Its aperture is exactly the size of a pinhole. (No wonder it's called a pinhole camera!) It allows only a little bit of light to shine on the film. So for the film to get enough light to form an image, the shutter has to stay open longer — at least a second. That's long enough for you to open and close the shutter by hand. Just like the fanciest cameras around, the pinhole camera gets the film, aperture, and shutter to work together to snap your "eye on the world."

PUT THE APERTURE, SHUTTER, AND BODY TOGETHER

Here's where making a pinhole camera gets a bit like making a sandwich.

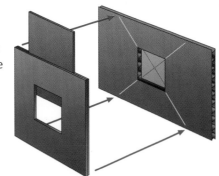

1 Use the diagonal lines on the aperture to center the aperture in the shutter window. Make sure the spacer is sandwiched between the aperture and shutter window.

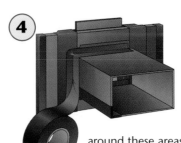

2 Glue the aperture to the shutter window like this. Put tape along the sides and bottom so no light can get in. Test the shutter. If it doesn't slide easily, trim it with the scissors.

3 Place the aperture face up on a table. To center the pinhole in the camera body, draw lines 1.15 cm ($\frac{15}{32}$ in) from both sides of the aperture holder and lines 0.8 cm ($\frac{5}{16}$ in) from the top and bottom. Put the camera body inside the center of this rectangle.

4 Tape the aperture to the body. Seal the inside and outside edges and corners with tape, so no light can get in. Go all around these areas again with another piece of tape. But do not put any tape in the way of the shutter slide. Look through the camera body to make sure no light is getting in.

Chilling with Desert TV

Who invented the pinhole camera? Nobody knows! But some people say it is over a thousand years old. Long ago in desert lands, or so the story goes, people would spend their afternoons in dark tents shaded from the sun. Sometimes light shining on a camel or a person who was passing by outside would be reflected through a small hole in the tent. Then the light would form an upside down image on the opposite wall of the tent. It was kind of like a desert TV!

ADD A VIEWFINDER

You can make a viewfinder out of a paper clip and a peephole out of a safety pin! The viewfinder will help you aim the camera. And the peephole will help line up the viewfinder with what you want to photograph.

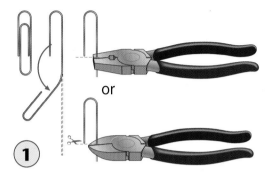

or

1

Put your safety goggles on. Get an adult to help use the wire cutters to cut the paper clip as you see here. Or use pliers to bend the leg back and forth until it breaks.

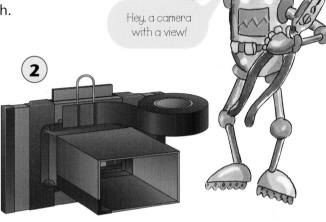

2

Tape the legs to the aperture holder, directly above the pinhole as you see here. The shutter will block out part of the viewfinder, but there should be enough left to see through.

Hey, a camera with a view!

Look Ma, No Lens!

Hey, how come the pinhole camera doesn't have a lens? A standard camera has a lens in front of the aperture. The lens is a large, specially shaped glass that directs light toward the film. To get a sharp and clear image on the film, the lens has to be focused by adjusting the distance between the aperture and the film. The pinhole camera doesn't need a lens, because the aperture is so small that all the light that passes through it is automatically focused onto the film. This automatic focus is like a free giveaway feature that comes with having a tiny pinhole. On the other hand, because the aperture is so small, very little light shines through. That's why the pinhole camera needs lots of outside light to take good shots!

Will you look at that? The lensless wonder snaps again!

③ To make the peephole, use the wire cutters to cut the unpointed leg of the safety pin as you see here. Ask an adult to help.

④ Use pliers to bend the legs of the pin as you see here, so the circle stands up in the middle.

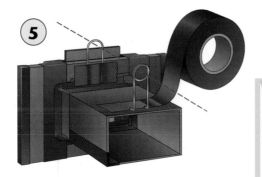

⑤ Place the circle on top of the camera body as you see here. Make sure the ends of the legs are pointing away from the edge. Tape the legs to hold the circle in place. Go to **Test This!**, below.

Want More Info? Surf the Web

Do a keyword search for "pinhole camera" in some of the search engines on the web and check out these sites:

www.nh.ultranet.com/~stewoody/

www.exploratorium.edu/science.Xexplorer/pringles.Xpinhole.html

www.pinhole.com

Test This!

Once you load the film, you won't be able to test the viewfinder. So do it now. Choose an object and aim the camera at it. Look through the peephole and line up the object with the viewfinder. Then check your aim by opening the shutter and looking through the pinhole to see if you can see the object. Remember to slide the shutter up to the shutter line and keep the camera still. Aim the camera at different objects. You'll notice it doesn't aim well at objects closer than 1.5 metres (5 ft). That's because the viewfinder and the aperture cannot be at the same place at the same time. So when you aim the viewfinder at a close object, the aperture points too low. But don't worry. Just tilt the camera up a bit for close objects.

LOAD THE FILM, ER, CAMERA!

Are you ready for this? You don't load the film into your pinhole camera. You load the camera into the film!

1 Put the open end of the camera body into the film cartridge. It should fit almost exactly with a 110 film cartridge.

2

Cover each of the four edges where the camera body and film cartridge meet with a piece of black tape. This will hold the film cartridge in place and shut out unwanted light.

3

Close the shutter to stop light from shining through the aperture and ruining the film. Way to go — you're ready to take some shots. All you have to do is advance the film, aim, and shoot!

Take Your Best Shot

How do the pros take their best shots? They practice — a lot! Then they know what results their equipment will deliver under different conditions. Be a pro. Practice taking pictures under different lighting conditions. Try leaving the shutter open for different amounts of time, too. For example, shoot an object by opening and closing the shutter as fast as you can. Then shoot the object with the shutter open for two seconds, four seconds, eight seconds, 16 seconds, and 32 seconds. Write down the picture number, the object, the lighting conditions, the film speed and type, and how long the shutter was open as in the chart below. Once your photos are developed, check the results you got from the different settings. And save your notes so you'll know what to do next time!

Photo #	Subject	Lighting	Shutter Time	Film Speed	Other Notes
1	Girl in playroom	Bright light through large window	8 sec.	ISO 100	Could only get her to stay still for a few seconds
2	Rocking horse	light through large window	2 min. 20 sec.	ISO 100	Tripod
3	Truck	light through large window	4 min. 40 sec.	ISO 100	Tripod Notice rocking horse for comparison

How to
Use Your Camera

Some things are just so...so...mechanical!

Advancing the Film

Advancing the film is tricky — but you'll be a pro at it in no time. See the little window on the back of the film cartridge? Numbers will appear in it to count the pictures as you advance the film. Each number will appear about four times.

Here's what to do:

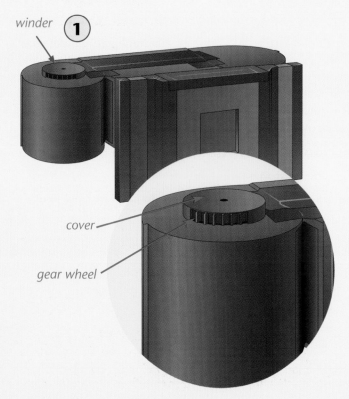

winder ①

cover

gear wheel

Find the film winder on the bottom of the large cylinder of the film cartridge. Look at the winder from the front of the camera. See that small gear wheel? That's what you use to advance the film.

②

Use the tip of a ballpoint pen to push the gear wheel counterclockwise. Push several times.

③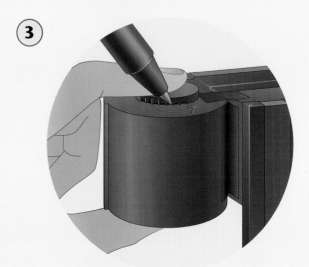

Does the gear wheel fling back? Stop it by using your fingers as a brake. After each time you push the gear, press the gear holder cover against the gear with your thumb and fingers.

Keep pushing and braking like this until you feel the tension of the film advancing. At first, you'll see lots of arrows in the window. Keep turning until you see the number 1. Stop turning when the second and third number 1s are both in the window at the same time.

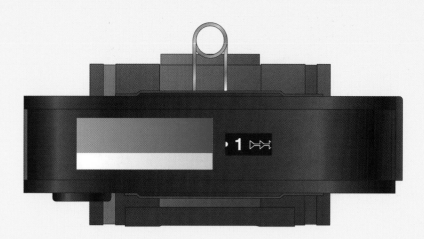

Setting Up the Shot

You'll get the best results from your pinhole camera outside on bright, sunny days. So make sure the object or scene you're shooting is well lit. If the camera moves while you're shooting, the shot will be blurry. To keep their cameras still while they shoot, pro photographers put them on a stand called a tripod. If you have a tripod, use it with elastic bands to hold the camera. Or else make your own stand by attaching the camera to the edge of a hardcover book with two elastic bands. Then put the book on a flat surface to take the shot.

Ready and Aim

Use the viewfinder to aim the camera. Look through the peephole, and point the camera so you can see the object or scene through the viewfinder's paper clip. Don't forget to tilt the camera up a bit when you're shooting objects that are less than 1.5 m (5 ft) away.

Snapping Shots

To take a picture, pull the shutter up to the marker line and then push it back down. Keep the camera still as you move the shutter. It's important to move it quickly so too much light doesn't get onto the film. On a bright sunny day, open the shutter for about eight seconds. If it's cloudy, open it for longer. Count the number of seconds by saying: one Mississippi, two Mississippi, and so on. Once you've snapped the shot, keep the shutter down until you're ready to take the next one. Or else you will ruin your photo.

Advancing the Film for Your Next Shot

Always advance the film after you take a shot, so the camera is ready for your next shot. Advance the film until you see the second and third copies of the next number in the window. When the film is finished, you will see Xs in the window. (Your film may have 12, 24, or 36 shots. The number of shots is listed on the package.) Then keep advancing until all the film is wound and the window goes blank or has diagonal lines.

Developing Your Film

Once you've taken all the pictures on the cartridge and wound the film to the end, take the tape off the cartridge and remove it. Now you need to get the film developed. Most camera and drug stores develop film and can have your photographs ready within a week. But not all of them develop cartridge film, so be prepared to try a few different places.

Take your best shot!

Buzz Off
Game

This game is a real buzz. You have to keep a cool head and a steady hand to move the wand along the wire as far as you can without touching the wire. Or else — bzzzt! —you'll set off the buzzer. Then it'll be time to buzz off and let your opponents take a turn.

Tools & Stuff You Need

- safety goggles
- wire cutters, wire stripper, pliers
- metal clothes hanger
- cardboard egg carton
- 2 C batteries
- 3-volt mini buzzer
- 13 Popsicle sticks, 2 elastic bands, 2 unpainted metal paper clips
- 2 butterfly clips 2.5 cm (1 in) long, masking tape, pen
- epoxy glue
- #22 or #24 gauge insulated wire 110 cm ($43\frac{1}{3}$ in) long
- electrical tape
- coarse sandpaper
- small nail
- 6 washers size 4 or 6
- metal washer, hole diameter 0.7 cm ($\frac{1}{4}$ in), outside diameter 1.6 cm ($\frac{5}{8}$ in), or slightly bigger

SHAPE UP THE HANGER

Don't buzz off. Hang around to turn a clothes hanger into a fun game!

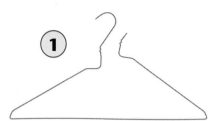

Wear your safety goggles for steps 1 to 4. Open the clothes hanger. Hold the hook in one hand and carefully untwist the neck with the other hand. Don't worry if the hook breaks off.

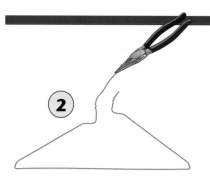

Use the pliers to straighten out the hook end of the hanger as shown.

Most hangers are painted or covered by a transparent coating that must be removed for electricity to flow through the hanger. Fold a small piece of sandpaper in half as shown.

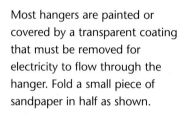

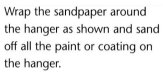

Wrap the sandpaper around the hanger as shown and sand off all the paint or coating on the hanger.

Use the pliers to bend the hanger into a cool shape as shown. Bend the hanger as many times as you want. But don't make the bends too sharp or the game will be too tough to play.

Life on the Wire

When it comes to live wire acts, the Flying Wallendas are the ones to watch. Members of this family of circus performers start performing death-defying high wire acts at the tender age of 11. In 1947, the Flying Wallendas began performing one of the most dangerous and certainly the most famous of high wire acts in the world — the Seven Person Pyramid. In the first level of the pyramid, four men stand on a high wire 7.6 m (25 ft) above the ground with two bars resting between their shoulders. In the second level, two men stand on those bars with a bar resting between their shoulders. Finally, balanced on that bar, a woman stands on a chair at the top of the pyramid. Whew! In 1962, a tragic accident made the Flying Wallendas stop doing the act for many years, but now they are performing it regularly again.

RIG UP THE CARTON

Here's an "eggcellent" way to turn an egg carton into a game box and a washer into an electric wand.

Use the wire cutters to cut a 1 m (3 ft) piece of wire.

2

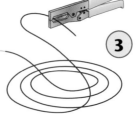

1 Turn the egg carton upside down. Use the small nail to poke a hole in the center of six egg holders exactly as shown.

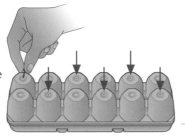

3 Use the wire stripper to strip 4.5 cm (1.5 in) of insulation from both ends of the wire. See stripping wire tips, page 59.

4

▶ Loop one end of the wire through the large washer twice and twist it.

▶ Use the pliers to tighten the twist and to press the wire against the washer so they make good contact. But be careful not to break the wire by twisting it too tightly.

5 Use the knife to gently saw a notch about 0.5 mm ($\frac{1}{50}$ in) deep and 3 mm ($\frac{1}{8}$ in) long at one end of each of two Popsicle sticks.

7 Use epoxy glue to glue the washer and wire to the tip of a notched Popsicle stick. Place the washer on the tip so the wire goes into the notch.

6 Use epoxy glue to glue a small washer over each hole on the egg holders. See epoxy glue tips, page 58. Let the epoxy dry while you do the next step. If the epoxy covers the holes once it's dry, use the small nail to poke through it after the next step.

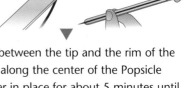

Leave a bit of space between the tip and the rim of the hole. Route the wire along the center of the Popsicle stick. Hold the washer in place for about 5 minutes until the epoxy hardens.

8

Once the epoxy is dry, use three small pieces of electrical tape to fasten the wire to the Popsicle stick.

Place the other notched Popsicle stick on top of the washer and wire glued to the first Popsicle stick as shown. Use three pieces of tape to hold the Popsicle sticks together, forming a washer-and-wire sandwich. Voilà! This is your wand!

9

MAKE A BATTERY PACK

Build a battery pack out of Popsicle sticks, elastic bands, and tape. It'll keep the batteries touching each other so that power can flow to the game.

Got all this stuff you need?

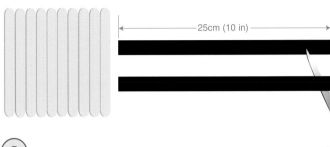

25cm (10 in)

1 Place 10 Popsicle sticks beside each other as shown. Cut two pieces of electrical tape about 25 cm (10 in) long.

2

4 cm (1½ in)

2.5 cm (1 in)

▲ Stick the tape on the Popsicle sticks, so 4 cm (1½ in) of tape is left on one side.

sticky side up

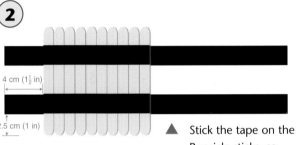

3 Turn over the Popsicle sticks, so the tape is sticky side up. Take out every second Popsicle stick.

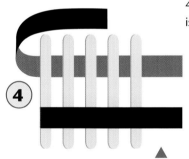

4

Put the long end of the tape over the Popsicle sticks. Press it down so it sticks to itself between the Popsicle sticks.

5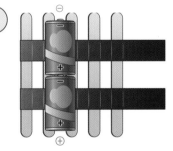

On a gap between two Popsicle sticks, stack the batteries as shown. Make sure the negative ⊖ terminal of one battery touches the positive ⊕ terminal of the other. Then line up the other ⊖ terminal with the top of the sticks.

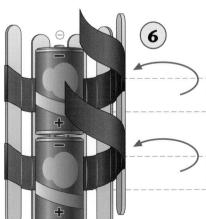

6 Wrap the Popsicle sticks tightly around the batteries as shown. Close up the battery pack with the tape.

7

Put two elastic bands around the battery pack as shown to keep the batteries in contact with each other.

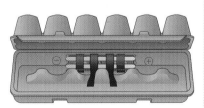

8 Use electrical tape to tape the battery pack in the egg carton as shown.

POWER UP

Wire up the circuit to add some power and some buzz.

1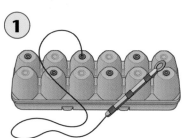
Feed the stripped end of the wand wire into the egg carton through one of the middle holes.

2 Loop the stripped end of the wire through a paper clip and twist it.

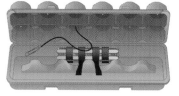

Use the pliers to tighten the twist and to press the wire onto the paper clip so they make good contact.

3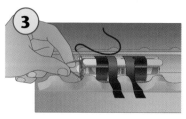
Slip the paper clip under the elastic bands on the ⊖ terminal of the battery pack. Make sure the paper clip touches the metal of the ⊖ terminal.

4 If the buzzer doesn't have wires, use the wire cutter to cut two 15 cm (6 in) pieces of wire. Then use the wire stripper to strip the insulation from all the ends. Loop one wire through each terminal and twist each wire. Use the pliers to tighten the twists as you did before.

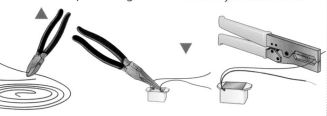

Use the wire stripper to strip 2.5 cm (1 in) of insulation from the end of each buzzer wire.

5
Check out the buzzer and its instructions to see which terminal is ⊕ (usually red) and which is ⊖ (usually black). On many buzzers it doesn't matter. Loop the ⊕ buzzer wire through the end of a paper clip and twist it. Use pliers to tighten the twist, so the wire makes good contact with the paper clip.

6
Slip the paper clip under the elastic bands on the ⊕ terminal of the battery pack. Go to **Test This!**, page 39.

When Lightning Strikes...

Around 1752, the world got all charged up about Benjamin Franklin's famous kite experiment. Franklin attached a wire to a kite and used it to conduct electricity from lightning to an electrical device. This showed that lightning is electricity conducted through the air from electrically charged storm clouds to the Earth. What's strange is that since then no one has figured out how to harness lightning and use it to power electrical devices. But scientists have been doing lots of work to make sure that lightning doesn't damage buildings and vehicles. To find ways to make sure that aircraft are safe from lightning, for example, they simulate lightning in labs and study how it strikes model airplanes. Then they can put important flight equipment away from areas where lightning may strike and make sure that lightning can't disrupt the equipment. Phew!

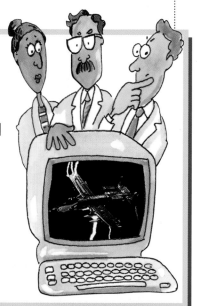

Test This!

What a buzz!

Check the connections you've made so far to make sure that they're working before you go on to the next part. Hold the wand and touch the washer against the stripped end of the unconnected $\ominus$ buzzer wire. Does it buzz? If so, hurray! Everything is working! If not, check that the $\oplus$ buzzer wire is connected to the $\oplus$ battery terminal. Also, check that the wand wire is connected to the $\ominus$ battery terminal. Then check that the wand wire is touching the washer and that all the wires are touching the paper clips that they're attached to. Inside the battery pack, check that the $\ominus$ terminal of one battery is pressing against the $\oplus$ terminal of the other battery. Now try the test again. If it still doesn't buzz, then the buzzer or the batteries need to be replaced.

GET CONNECTED

Make some important connections to get this game together.

1

Make a connection wire. Use the wire cutters to cut a 15 cm (6 in) piece of wire.

Use the wire stripper to strip 2.5 cm (1 in) of insulation from each end.

3 Connect the other end of the connection wire to one metal handle of a butterfly clip. Loop the wire end through the clip twice and twist it.

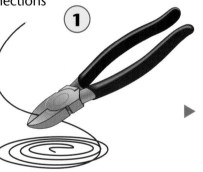

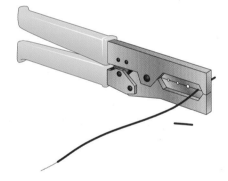

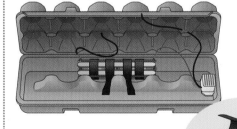

2

Lengthen the $\ominus$ buzzer wire by adding the connection wire to it. Twist together the stripped end of the $\ominus$ buzzer wire and a stripped end of the connection wire. Cover the twist with electrical tape.

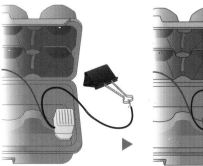

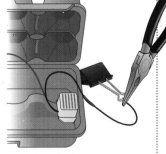

Use the pliers to tighten the twist, so the wire and the clip handle make good contact. Go to **Test This!**, page 40.

Test This!

Test the connections you've just made. Touch the washer on the wand to the butterfly clip handle. Does it buzz? If it does, everything is A-OK! If it doesn't buzz, make sure the clip handles are metal and not painted. Check that the ⊖ buzzer wire is touching the connection wire. Then check that the other end of the connection wire is touching the butterfly clip. Then try the test again.

Buzz me. It's working!

4 Feed one end of the hanger into the egg carton through the washer as shown.

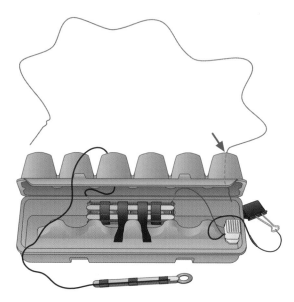

5 Clip the butterfly clip onto the end of the hanger as shown.

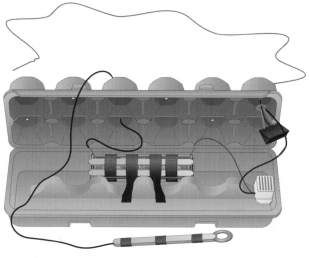

6 Flip up the butterfly clip handles so they touch the hanger as shown. Go to **Test This!**, page 41.

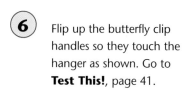

Test This!

Test the connections you've just made. Touch the washer on the end of the wand to the hanger. Does the buzzer buzz? If so, the connections are working perfectly! If not, check that the butterfly clip and its handles are touching the hanger. Also, check that all of the paint or transparent coating has been removed from the hanger around the areas where the butterfly clip handles and the wand are touching it. Then try the test again.

Stick around — so you can Buzz Off!

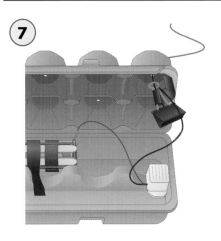

7

Once the buzzer is buzzing, tightly wrap electrical tape around the clip handles to hold the hanger in place.

BUZZ ON, BUZZ OFF!

Hey, don't buzz off yet. Get set for a noisy couple of steps.

1

Put the free end of the hanger into the washer on the wand. Noisy, huh?

2

Put the free end of the hanger into the egg carton through the washer as shown.

3

Inside the carton, attach a butterfly clip to the end of the hanger as shown.

4

Flip up the butterfly clip handles and tape them tightly around the hanger with the electrical tape.

5

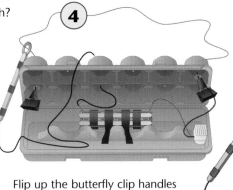

Now let's stop that crazy buzzing! Close the egg carton. To make a "buzz off" switch that stops electricity from flowing from the hanger to the wand, wrap electrical tape around a small section of the hanger as shown. Then slide the wand so the washer is on the tape.

FINISHING TOUCHES

Pack the game in the carton and get set to play it.

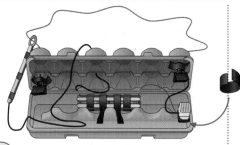

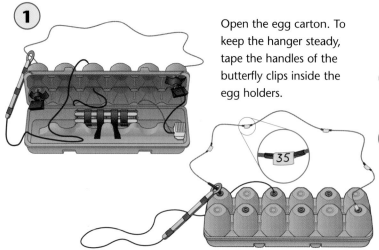

1 Open the egg carton. To keep the hanger steady, tape the handles of the butterfly clips inside the egg holders.

2 Tape the buzzer as shown to hold it in place.

3 Close the carton. After each major bend in the hanger, wrap a small piece of electrical tape around the hanger. Put small bits of masking tape on the electrical tape and label the masking tape with numbers of points as shown.

HOW TO PLAY BUZZ OFF

You can play Buzz Off with your friends or all on your own.

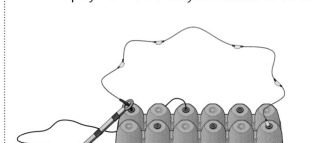

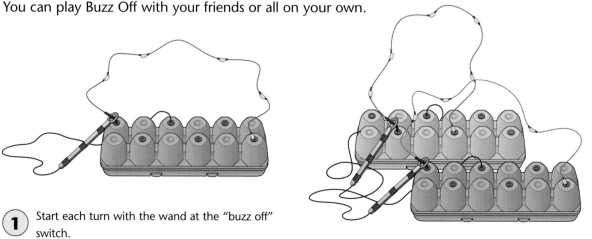

1 Start each turn with the wand at the "buzz off" switch.

2 On his or her turn, each player moves the wand along the hanger as far as possible without touching the hanger. As the wand passes each tape marker, the player adds the number of points on the marker to his or her score. The object of the game is to get as many points as possible.

3 If the wand touches the hanger and the buzzer goes off, the player's turn is over.

4 After 5 turns each, the player who has the most points wins the game.

5 When you're ready for a new challenge, remove the hanger, bend it differently and feed it through different washer holes in the egg carton.

6 Once you've bent the hanger into a new shape, reconnect it by redoing steps 5 to 7 in Get Connected, steps 1 to 4 in Buzz On, Buzz Off!, and Step 1 in Finishing Touches.

Zoom In
on the Mechanics

What makes the wire buzz when the wand touches it? Electricity! Electricity flows from the batteries to the buzzer. Here's how: the game is made out of a buzzer circuit, or pathway for electricity to travel on. Electricity must flow in a loop. The buzzer is connected to the ⊕ terminal of the battery pack and to the hanger, while the wand is connected to the ⊖ terminal of the battery pack. Like this, the loop is incomplete. But when the wand touches the wire, it completes the loop and electricity flows from the batteries to the buzzer and the buzzer buzzes. The Buzz Off switch that "turns off" the buzzer works in the same kind of way. Made out of electrical tape wrapped around the hanger, it breaks the loop by preventing the wand from touching the hanger.

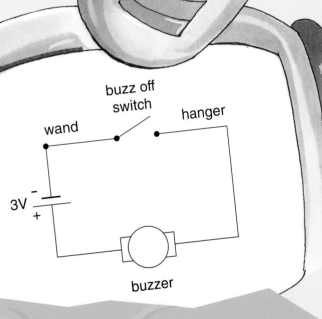

Surf the Web

Want to find more information about lightning and Benjamin Franklin's famous kite experiment? Do keyword searches for "lightning" and "Benjamin Franklin" in some search engines on the Internet.

Cool
Shades

These shades are so cool, you can even wear them in the dark. Make the lights on them flash slowly to look spooky or speed them up to look flashy— whatever suits your mood. Wear them to parties. Or use them to light up a mask or toy. You can even hide them under your bed to keep scary monsters away!

Electronic parts like these come in packs of more than one. So shop with a friend and share the parts. Bring this book along to show salespeople what you're looking for.

Tools & Stuff You Need

- safety goggles
- 9-volt rectangular battery and battery snap connector
- small two-terminal SPST switch
- 7 carbon film resistors: 4 47K Ohm resistors, a 100K Ohm resistor, a 100 Ohm resistor, a 4700 Ohm resistor
- 22 microfarad electrolytic capacitor
- integrated circuit #1458
- NPN transistor #2N3904
- 2 LEDs 1.6 to 2.2 volts with long leads

- sunglasses or eyeglass frames
- 270 cm (106 in) of solid-core breadboard wire #22 or #24 gauge
- small electronic breadboard and small cardboard box big enough to hold the breadboard
- scissors, tape; contact cement or epoxy glue
- hole punch
- needle-nose pliers, wire cutters, wire stripper

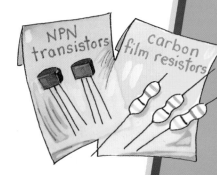

Time for a "haircut." Cut the leads on the resistors and the capacitor to get them ready for action.

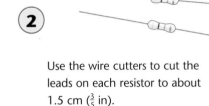

(1)

Wear your safety goggles for steps 1 and 2. Use the wire cutters to cut the capacitor leads to about 1.5 cm ($\frac{3}{5}$ in).

(2)

Use the wire cutters to cut the leads on each resistor to about 1.5 cm ($\frac{3}{5}$ in).

Building Tips

Pssst. Want to build the cool shades with no hassles? Read this.

- When you're not using the electronic parts, keep them in their packages. This will help you remember what they are and protect them from damage.
- When you put a part on the breadboard, make sure its leads don't touch the leads of any other part, or the circuit won't work properly and the parts may get damaged.
- Connect all the electronic parts exactly as shown. Wrong connections can damage the parts. Make sure the integrated circuit, transistor, capacitor, battery, LEDs face the same way they do in the book.
- Don't shock the parts. Before you start working with the electronics, touch a water faucet, TV, or computer case to get rid of any little shocks on your body. This will "discharge" your body on something safe, so you don't "discharge" on a part, which may damage it.

ADD THE LIGHT GEAR

Add some Lit-up LEDs to your shades.

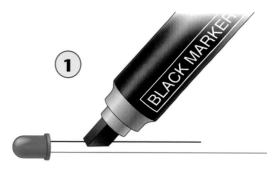

1

Check out the instructions that came with the LEDs to see which LED lead is negative ⊖. It's usually the shorter lead. Color this lead on both LEDs to help you identify it later.

2

Use the pliers to carefully bend all the LED leads as shown.

3

Use the pliers to bend the ⊕ LED lead, on the left, as shown.

4

Loop and bend the ⊖ lead through the ⊕ lead as shown.

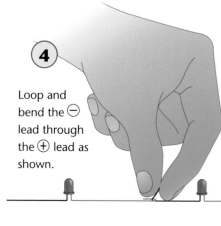

5

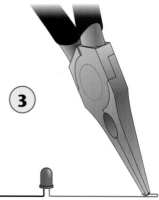

With your fingers or pliers, squish the leads tightly together so they make a good connection. Carefully bend the LED bulbs so that they are both pointing the same way upwards.

6

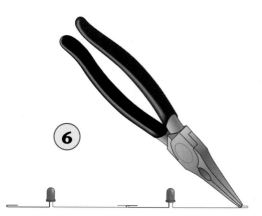

Use the pliers to bend the end of each outside lead into a small loop as shown.

Wire up the shades so you can power them up.

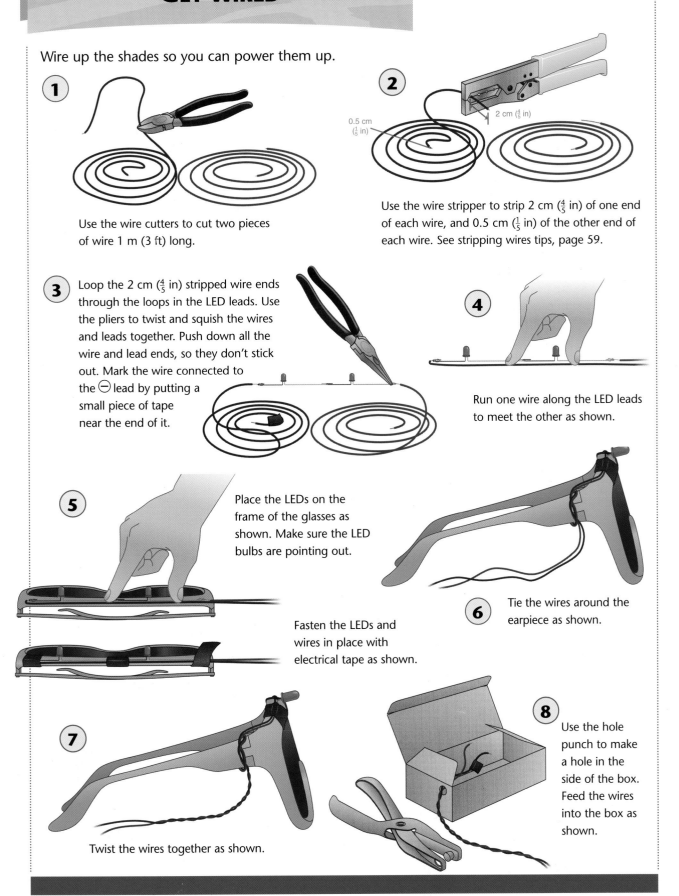

1 Use the wire cutters to cut two pieces of wire 1 m (3 ft) long.

2 Use the wire stripper to strip 2 cm ($\frac{4}{5}$ in) of one end of each wire, and 0.5 cm ($\frac{1}{5}$ in) of the other end of each wire. See stripping wires tips, page 59.

0.5 cm ($\frac{1}{5}$ in)

2 cm ($\frac{4}{5}$ in)

3 Loop the 2 cm ($\frac{4}{5}$ in) stripped wire ends through the loops in the LED leads. Use the pliers to twist and squish the wires and leads together. Push down all the wire and lead ends, so they don't stick out. Mark the wire connected to the ⊖ lead by putting a small piece of tape near the end of it.

4 Run one wire along the LED leads to meet the other as shown.

5 Place the LEDs on the frame of the glasses as shown. Make sure the LED bulbs are pointing out.

Fasten the LEDs and wires in place with electrical tape as shown.

6 Tie the wires around the earpiece as shown.

7 Twist the wires together as shown.

8 Use the hole punch to make a hole in the side of the box. Feed the wires into the box as shown.

POWER UP THE BREADBOARD

Outfit the breadboard with a battery and an on-and-off switch.

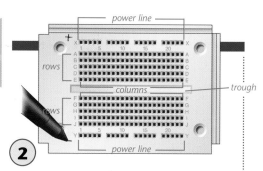

(1) Snap the battery connector onto the battery as shown. Most connectors have a black wire and a red wire. The black wire connects to the $\ominus$ battery terminal and the red wire to the $\oplus$ terminal. Strip 1.5 cm ($\frac{3}{5}$ in) from the end of the red $\oplus$ wire.

(2) Take a good look at the breadboard. It's made to connect wires and electrical parts. Check out its rows, columns, power lines, and trough and label them as shown to help you identify them later. Note that each hole corresponds with a row letter and column number. See breadboard on page 60 in the glossary for how to put components in the breadboard.

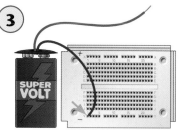

(3) Put the black $\ominus$ wire from the battery connector into the $\ominus$ power line as shown. Gently press the wire into the hole so about 0.5 cm ($\frac{1}{5}$ in) of it goes into the hole.

If the black wire doesn't fit into the hole easily, cut a 10 cm (4 in) piece of wire. Strip one end 1.5 cm ($\frac{3}{5}$ in) and the other end 0.5 cm ($\frac{1}{5}$ in).

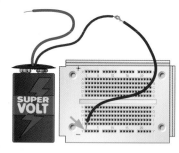

Use pliers to twist and squish the 1.5 cm ($\frac{3}{5}$ in) stripped wire and the black wire together. Then gently press the other end of the wire into the hole.

Zoom In
on the Mechanics

Check out the "What's That?" Glossary and follow this circuit diagram as you build.

Electronics are at the heart of TV, radio, stereo, computers, robotics, space ships…. When pros are inventing new devices and experimenting with a new circuit, they make a circuit diagram and then wire it up on a breadboard, just like you do to make your Cool Shades. The breadboard is designed so that you can easily place and remove wires and components — like the transistor, IC chip, capacitor, and resistors. Once the pros have tested and are happy with their breadboard circuit, they have the circuit printed on a Printed Circuit Board (PCB), with copper printed lines for wires, and holes for the components's pins and leads to fit into. Many copies can be made of a PCB. Peek inside any electronic equipment and you will see a circuit a lot like the one you are building — but don't touch the components!

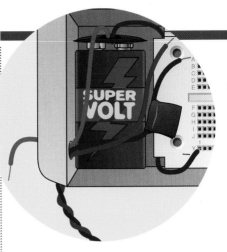

 4
Put the battery and breadboard in the box as shown. Feed the red ⊕ battery wire out of the box through the same hole as the LED wires.

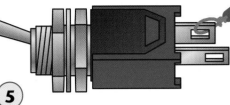

5
Connect the red ⊕ battery wire to one of the switch terminals. Loop and twist it onto the terminal. See connecting wires tips, page 58.

 6
Use the wire cutters to cut a 10 cm (4 in) connection wire. Use the wire stripper to strip 2.5 cm (1 in) from one end and 0.5 cm ($\frac{1}{5}$ in) from the other.

7
Connect the 2.5 cm (1 in) stripped end to the switch. Loop and twist it through the free switch terminal as shown.

8
Wrap electrical tape around each wire connected to the switch as shown to insulate the connections. Feed the other end of the connection wire through the hole into the box.

 9
Put the free end of the connection wire into the ⊕ Power Line on the breadboard as shown.

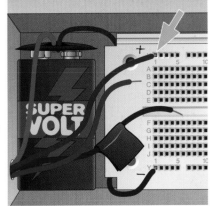

10
Use the contact cement or epoxy glue to glue the switch to the box as shown.

LIGHT IT UP

Hook up the LEDs and get all lit up.

Use the wire stripper to strip 0.5 cm ($\frac{1}{5}$ in) insulation from all the ends of the wires.

1 Use the wire cutters to cut 9 pieces of connection wire 5 cm (2 in) long.

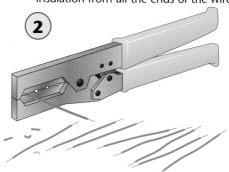

2

Use the pliers to carefully bend the leads of the 100 Ohm resistor into a U shape. See resistors in the glossary, page 62.

3

4 Put one resistor lead in Column 8 Row A and the other in Column 10 Row A as shown. Line up the leads with the holes. Then gently push the leads down, so about 0.5 cm ($\frac{1}{5}$ in) of them go into the holes. Part of the leads and the resistor will sit above the board. Don't worry if the leads bend a bit.

5 Connect the ⊕ wire from the LEDs to the resistor by placing it in 10B (Column 10 Row B).

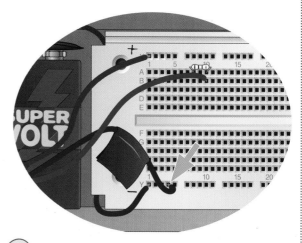

6 Put the ⊖ wire from the LEDs into the ⊖ Power Line as shown. Go to **Test This!**, page 51.

Test This!

Test out what you've built so far.

- On the breadboard, put a small connection wire in 8B to connect it to the resistor. Remember to remove this wire when you have finished testing.
- Put the other end of the wire into the ⊕ Power Line to power up the circuit.
- Did the LEDs go on? If so, everything is working! Skip the rest of the steps below.
- If not, flip the switch. If the LEDs come on, congrats! Take a building break and skip the steps below.
- If they still don't come on, carefully check all the connections. Go back through all the steps and make sure that the ⊕ and ⊖ wires have not been mixed up. Also, check that the stripped wires go deep into the breadboard holes and make good contact.
- If they don't come on now, one of the LEDs or the battery needs to be replaced.

The guys gotta see this!

ADD THE TRANSISTOR

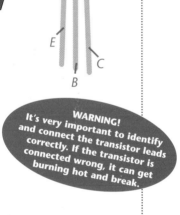

Put the transistor into the breadboard to make the LEDs flash on and off. Ooh, cool!

1

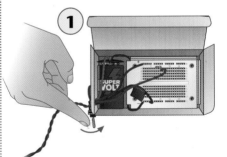

Flip the switch to OFF.

2

Check out the transistor. It has three leads. When the flat side of the transistor is facing you as shown, the left lead is E (emitter), the middle is B (base) and the right lead is C (collector).

WARNING! It's very important to identify and connect the transistor leads correctly. If the transistor is connected wrong, it can get burning hot and break.

3

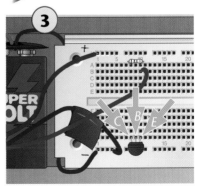

Place the transistor on the breadboard. Put the E lead in 10J, B lead in 9J, and the C lead in 8J. Make sure the correct leads are in the correct holes.

4

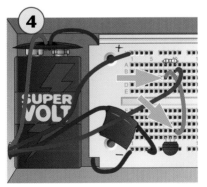

To connect the E transistor lead to the resistor, put one end of a connection wire in 10J, and the other end in 8C.

5 To connect the C transistor lead to the ⊕ battery terminal, put one end of a connection wire in 8F, and the other end in the ⊕ Power Line.

8-PIN
MINI-DIP

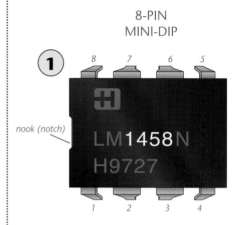

①

nook (notch)

LM**1458**N
H9727

Check out the integrated circuit (IC) chip. See the nook on its left side? When the nook is in this position, the pins on the IC are numbered as shown. Turn your IC, so the nook is in this position.

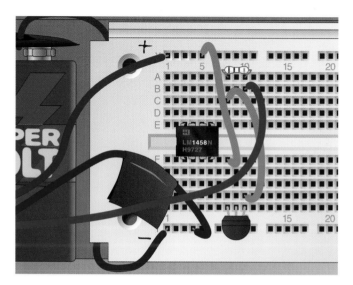

② Put the IC on the breadboard. Line up the IC pins with the breadboard's holes exactly as shown, making sure the IC straddles the trough. Gently push the IC down, so all the pins go into the holes at once. ▶

Let Colors Do the Talking

What's up with the color codes on resistors? Since resistors are too small for words to be readable on them, the color codes tell you the strength of the resistor. Color codes are used to communicate many other things, too. Ships, for example, have a flag bag of color-coded Signal Flags to send important messages to nearby ships. This is especially important if the ship's radio breaks down, or if the crew isn't allowed to use its radio because they're involved in a secret mission. This colorful language of the sea can spell out messages, letter by letter, or be flown in combination to send special meanings. For instance, if you were sailing towards the flags here, they'd be telling you you're "running into danger" from a "h-u-n-g-r-y" sea monster!

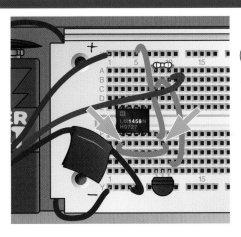

3 To connect the B transistor lead to Pin 1, put one end of a small connection wire in 9G, and the other end in 3G.

4 To connect Pin 3 to an unused column, put one end of a connection wire in 5I, and the other end in 7H.

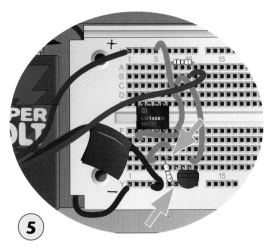

5 To connect a 47K Ohm resistor from Pin 3 to the ⊖ battery terminal, put one resistor lead in 7I, and the other lead in the ⊖ Power Line as shown. See resistors in the glossary, page 62.

6 To connect a 47K Ohm resistor from Pin 3 to the ⊕ battery terminal, put one resistor lead in 7F, and the other lead in 8H.

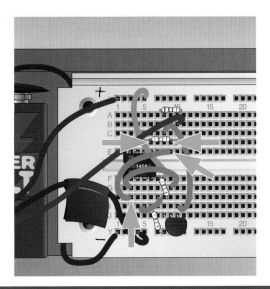

7 To connect a 47K Ohm resistor between Pin 5 and Pin 1, put one resistor lead in 6D and the other lead in 9D. Then put one end of a connection wire in 9E, and the other end in 3H.

SET THAT SPOOKY FREQUENCY

Add a capacitor and resistor to set the rate at which the LEDs flash.

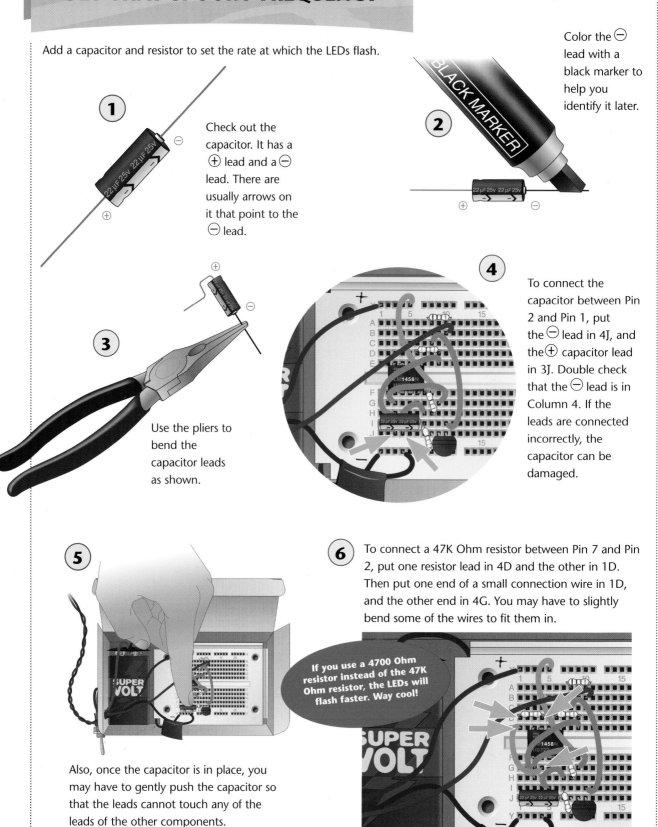

1 Check out the capacitor. It has a ⊕ lead and a ⊖ lead. There are usually arrows on it that point to the ⊖ lead.

2 Color the ⊖ lead with a black marker to help you identify it later.

3 Use the pliers to bend the capacitor leads as shown.

4 To connect the capacitor between Pin 2 and Pin 1, put the ⊖ lead in 4J, and the ⊕ capacitor lead in 3J. Double check that the ⊖ lead is in Column 4. If the leads are connected incorrectly, the capacitor can be damaged.

5 Also, once the capacitor is in place, you may have to gently push the capacitor so that the leads cannot touch any of the leads of the other components.

6 To connect a 47K Ohm resistor between Pin 7 and Pin 2, put one resistor lead in 4D and the other in 1D. Then put one end of a small connection wire in 1D, and the other end in 4G. You may have to slightly bend some of the wires to fit them in.

If you use a 4700 Ohm resistor instead of the 47K Ohm resistor, the LEDs will flash faster. Way cool!

POWER UP THE IC CHIP

Get it together and make things work with a few final connections.

1

To connect a 100K Ohm resistor between Pin 5 and Pin 7, put one lead in 6B, and the other in 4B.

2

To connect Pin 6 to Pin 3, put one end of a connection wire in 5D, and the other end in 5H.

3

To power the IC at Pin 8, put one end of a connection wire in 3A, and the other end in the $\oplus$ Power Line.

4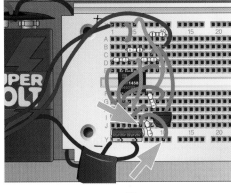

To connect Pin 4 to the $\ominus$ battery terminal, put one end of a connection wire in 6J, and the other end in the $\ominus$ Power Line. Go to **Test This!**, below.

Test This!

Test out your cool shades before you put on the finishing touches.

- Before you switch on the LEDs, make sure none of the leads on any electrical parts is touching the leads of any other electrical part and that all of the wires are well placed in the holes.
- Flip the switch on. Do the LEDs slowly turn on and slowly turn off? If so, way to go! Everything is working perfectly. Skip the steps below.
- If not, carefully check all the connections by going back over all the steps since the last **Test This!**, page 51.
- Check that the transistor, IC, and capacitor are correctly positioned on the breadboard, with the correct leads and pins in the correct holes.
- Make sure the switch is properly connected to the battery and the $\oplus$ Power Line.
- Make sure the $\ominus$ battery terminal is well connected to the $\ominus$ Power Line.

Too cool for words!

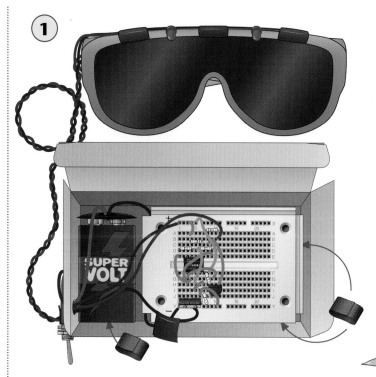

1

Make sure the breadboard and the battery are right inside the box. Carefully secure them with tape, so they don't move around and the wires and parts don't get pulled out. Make sure the tape touches only the battery and the back of the breadboard.

2

Close the box. Put on the shades. Or put them on a stuffed animal, doll, or mask. Or put them under your bed one night and check out little brother's reaction!

3

When you wear the shades, you can carry the box, attach it to your belt, put it in your pocket, or stuff it under your hat.

In the Eye of the Chameleon

When it comes to eyeing a meal, the chameleon is one cool customer. This tropical lizard, known for its remarkable ability to change the color of its skin, has big round eyes that can see all the way around without the creature ever moving its head. Spooky, or what?! Each of the chameleon's eyes can move independently of the other. So one eye can look forward while the other looks back. That means nearby bugs had better watch out if they don't want to be snatched up as dinner. And they do. Most insects have compound eyes made of hundreds of lenses that can look in all directions at once. It's enough to make you go bug-eyed!

How-to Tips

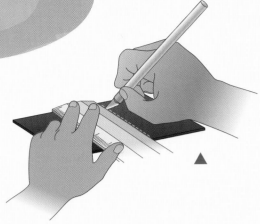

DRILLING, AND CUTTING WITH X-ACTO KNIVES AND BLADES

Always have an adult help you to use a drill or to cut anything that needs an X-Acto knife or sharp blade. Don't try to cut through a bunch of thick things at once. Put some newspaper underneath the material you're cutting to protect the table or area you're cutting on.

Cut away from your body and your hands — never cut toward them. To make a cut, put light pressure on the blade. Then pull the blade across the material. Go over the cut with the X-Acto knife until the material is cut all the way through.

GLUING

Try not to get glue everywhere as you use it. The step-by-step building instructions for each gadget will tell you if you need to wait for the glue to dry before you do the next step. The instructions will also tell you what type of glue to use. Regular white or brown glue works well for paper. But when you need to glue other things together, contact cement or 5-minute epoxy glue usually works better. Ask an adult for help. To use contact cement or 5-minute epoxy glue safely and correctly, follow the directions on their packages and these tips:

Contact cement works well when the things you need to glue together have similar surfaces.

• Contact Cement

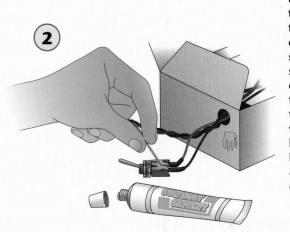

Use a Popsicle stick or toothpick to spread a thin coat of contact cement onto the surfaces you want to stick together. Be careful not to apply too much. Otherwise, the contact cement will not dry and it will become like toffee. Leave the pieces apart and let the contact cement dry for about 15 minutes.

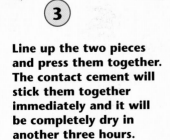

Line up the two pieces and press them together. The contact cement will stick them together immediately and it will be completely dry in another three hours.

• Epoxy Glue

Epoxy glue is good for gluing together things that have different surfaces. You can use it to make a small pool of glue around the two surfaces. As this pool of glue dries, it will become hard like plastic.

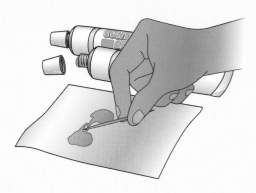

Epoxy glue usually comes in two tubes: one has sticky stuff and the other has hardener. On a piece of foil, squeeze equal small amounts out of each tube as shown. Mix them together with a Popsicle stick or toothpick.

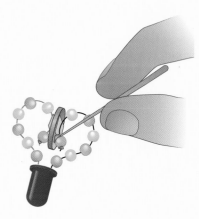

Use a Popsicle stick or toothpick to apply the mixed epoxy glue to the two surfaces you want to stick together.

Hold the pieces together for about five minutes until the epoxy glue hardens. It will take about 24 hours for it to dry completely.

CONNECTING WIRES

To connect two wires, you need to join the metal of the wires together.

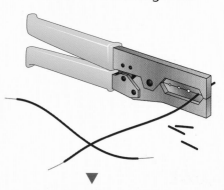

Strip about 2.5 cm (1 in) of the plastic covering from one end of each wire. See wire stripping tips, facing page.

Tightly twist the metal of the wires together. Cover the twist with electrical tape or a special plastic connector cap if you have one around. But do not use Scotch tape, masking tape, or any other nonelectrical tape, because the wires may heat up. Wrap electrical tape around the twist several times and cover the entire part of the stripped wire.

SPLITTING SPEAKER WIRES

Speaker wire is like a double wire. It is made of two wires that are attached side by side. The plastic covering on the wires joins them together, but the metal of the two wires does not touch.

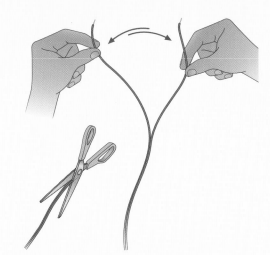

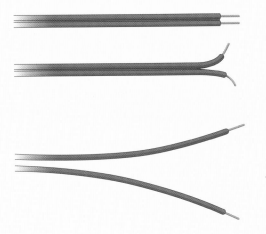

▲ To split speaker wire, cut the end with scissors and then pull the wires apart with your hands.

◄ In some gadgets, speaker wire is used with its two halves attached. In others, its ends are split. And in others, its two halves are split apart completely and used separately the same as single wires.

STRIPPING WIRES

The goal of wire stripping is to remove the plastic covering from the wire without cutting the metal of the wire. It's pretty tricky and takes lots of practice.

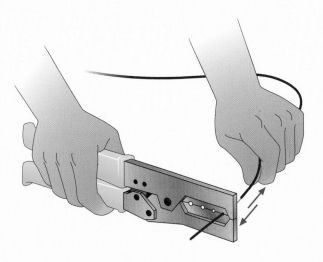

Most pliers have a wire stripper at the end of their jaws near where the handles join. If you don't have a wire stripper, you can use a nail clipper.

To strip a wire, place about 2.5 cm (1 in) of the end of it between the blades of the wire stripper or nail clippers. Lightly squeeze the handle so the blades cut only the plastic. Release the pressure a bit. Then pull the blades toward the end of the wire to remove the plastic.

battery: a device that changes chemical energy into electrical energy. Batteries come in many different sizes and shapes that supply different amounts of energy.

blinking LED: a special kind of light-emitting diode that blinks; see LED

breadboard: what the pros use to invent new devices. The breadboard is designed so that you can easily place and remove components and wires; it can be reused for different electronic projects. It is made up of rows, columns, troughs, $\oplus$ power line, and $\ominus$ power line. Each hole is identified by its row letter and column number.

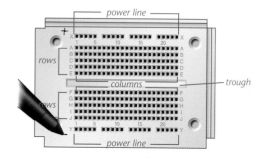

• column: inside the breadboard, all the holes in the same column are connected to each other until you get to either a power line or a trough. The holes on any one column are not connected to the holes on any other column.

• row: the holes in the same row are not connected to each other

• trough: a blank row on the board without any holes. The holes in the same column on either side of the trough are not connected to each other.

• power lines: separate lines of holes on the top and bottom (or sometimes on the far right and left). All of the holes in this line are connected to each other.

To place components on the breadboard, line up the leads (sometimes called legs or pins) of the component with the specified holes and gently press so that about 0.5 cm ($\frac{1}{5}$ in) of each lead goes into the hole. The rest of the lead and the component should sit above the board. To place a component with long leads, use pliers to bend the leads so that they will fit from hole to hole.

breaking contact: when materials that do not conduct electricity interrupt the flow of electricity through a contact

buzzer: a device that makes a buzzing sound. You may find many different types of buzzers at your local electronic store. Any one of them is fine for the gadgets in this book except for a printed-circuit (pc) mounted one. Make sure the buzzer is 3-volt DC and that it has two terminals with wires so you can connect it to a circuit. If the buzzer has two terminals but no wires, you can still use it — strip the ends of two 15 cm (6 in) long wires and connect one to each terminal. See stripping and connecting wires tips, pages 58 and 59.

chemical reaction: a change in which one or more substances form new substances by breaking down, mixing with other substances, or changing parts with other substances

circuit: a path that electric current can flow on

Symbols Used in Circuit Diagrams

 Connected Wire

 Crossing Wires (not connected)

 LED (Flashy Jewelry, Outta Sight Light Box, Cool Shades)

 Battery (Flashy Jewelry, Outta Sight Light Box, Buzz Off Game, Cool Shades)

 *Buzzer (Buzz Off Game)*

 Switch (Cool Shades)

 Resistor (Cool Shades)

 Transistor (Cool Shades)

 Electrolytic Capacitor (Cool Shades)

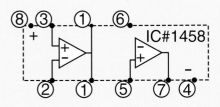

IC Chip (Cool Shades)

circuit diagram: a road map of the electrical connections needed to build a circuit. The lines that join parts together in a circuit diagram show that those parts are connected by a wire or by being twisted together. The length and position of these lines are not accurate. A circuit diagram shows only the connections and the order of connections.

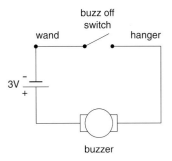

In a circuit diagram, standard symbols, like the ones shown at left, stand for electrical parts.

conduct: to transmit, or send, electrical energy

connection: the attachment of two or more things that conduct electricity so electricity can flow from one to the other(s)

contact: a point where two pieces of metal touch so electric current can flow from one to the other. Plastic, paper, glue, and paint can stop electricity from flowing through a contact; see breaking contact. So be careful not to get them on contacts as you build the gadgets.

electric current: the flow of electricity

electrolytic capacitor: a component that stores a small amount of electric charge and releases this electricity at a later time at a controlled rate, like a small rechargeable battery. The capacitance, or number of microfarads (μF), is written on the cylinder. It is very important when connecting an electrolytic capacitor that the ⊖ and ⊕ leads are connected in the correct direction. Otherwise the capacitor may be damaged.

film speed: all photographic film has a speed or ASA number that's marked on the package after the letters ISO. The higher the number is, the faster the film. Fast film needs less light to record a picture than slow film: given the same lighting conditions and aperture size, fast film takes less time to record a picture, so the shutter does not have to be open for as long. For example, 110 cartridge film comes in ISO 100, ISO 200, and ISO 400. ISO 200 is twice as fast as ISO 100, and ISO 400 is twice as fast as ISO 200. That means that if the perfect exposure time for a photo is 1 second at ISO 200, it would be 2 seconds at ISO 100, and 1/2 second at ISO 400.

gauge: the thickness of a wire. The gauge number measures the diameter of the wire. For the gadgets in this book, 18 to 22 gauge wire is best. The lower the gauge number, the thicker the wire. So 18 gauge wire is thicker than 22 gauge wire.

insulation: the plastic covering on wires

integrated circuit chip: also called an IC chip, a single electronic component made up of many (possibly millions) of electronic parts; it is used to replace large circuits by a single component.

integrated circuit chip

key: a guide for encoding and decoding secret messages

keyword: an important word to use in an Internet search

LED: a light-emitting diode. You can find LEDs in your local electronic store or the electronic department of your local hardware store. Try to get LEDs that have long leads — 3 cm ($1\frac{1}{8}$ in). If you need lots of LEDs to make your gadgets, it will usually cost less to buy packs of LEDs rather than individual LEDs.

mechanism: a group of parts that act like a machine

motor: a machine that changes electrical energy into mechanical energy

negative: see terminal

positive: see terminal

power: energy to do work

resistor: a device that cuts down the electrical power that flows through a system. The rate at which it cuts down power is measured in ohms. Carbon-film resistors are beige colored, shaped like a sausage, and have 3 or 4 colored stripes. The number of ohms in the resistor, which is called its resistance, is coded on the resistor by the arrangement of colored stripes.

When you are building, it is important to use the right resistors with the correct resistance. To read the code in the colored stripes, hold the resistor so that the silver stripe, gold stripe, or blank space is on the right side, and read the stripes from left to right. The first two stripes tell you the number. Find the colors of the first two stripes in the chart below and look in the Number column: for example, brown-black would be 1 and 0, to give you 10; yellow-violet would be 4 and 7, to give you 47. The third stripe gives you the multiplier. Find the color of the third stripe in the chart below and look in the Multiplier column: for example, brown would be 10; orange would be 1000 (or 1K). Now multiply the number by the multiplier to give you the resistance: for example, brown-black-brown would be 10 x 10 = 100 Ohms; yellow-violet-orange would be 47 x 1000 = 47 000 (called 47K) Ohms.

Color stripes	Number it represents	Multiplier
Black	0	X 1
Brown	1	X 10
Red	2	X 100
Orange	3	X 1000 (1K)
Yellow	4	X 10 000 (10K)
Green	5	X 100 000 (100K)
Blue	6	X 1 000 000 (1M)
Violet	7	(colors not used as
Gray	8	multipliers)
Other: Gold, Silver, or Blank	4th stripe only, represents the accuracy of the resistance value	

speaker wire: is like a double wire. It's made of two wires that are attached side by side. Its plastic covering joins the wires together, but the metal of the two wires does not touch. Speaker wire is the recommended wire for the gadgets in this book. Although you can use other electrical wire, speaker costs less, and the most inexpensive kind works well for these gadgets.

switch: an electric device that turns something on or off. You can make many of the switches required for the gadgets in this book, but you will need to buy a few. You will find lots of different switches with different button styles and numbers of terminals at your local electronic store. An SPST switch, which is needed for the cool shades on page 44, is a "single pole, single throw" switch. That's just a way of saying that it has two terminals and it switches one circuit on or off.

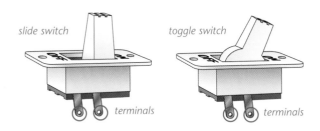

slide switch　　　*toggle switch*

terminals　　　*terminals*

terminal: a place or wire on a device such as a battery, buzzer, or lightbulb where an electrical connection is made or broken so the device can get or give power. Sometimes terminals and terminal wires are called contact points or connectors. They're usually marked positive ⊕ or negative ⊖ to show how they should be connected. The step-by-step instructions for building the gadgets say what to connect to the ⊕ and ⊖ terminals.

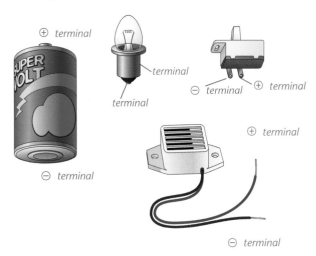

⊕ *terminal*

terminal

⊖ *terminal*　⊕ *terminal*

terminal

⊖ *terminal*

⊕ *terminal*

⊖ *terminal*

transistor: a component that regulates and changes the flow of electricity through a circuit. When using a transistor, make sure you connect it according to instructions; a wrongly connected transistor can heat up and be damaged.

volt: the unit used to measure the amount of electricity between two terminals in a circuit

Index